THE MOST INSPIRATIONAL WOMEN'S FOOTBALL STORIES OF ALL TIME

FOR TEENAGE GIRLS!

MICHAEL LANGDON

Copyright © 2024 by Michael Langdon

All rights reserved.

No part of this book may be reproduced in any form or by any electronic or mechanical means, including information storage and retrieval systems, without written permission from the author, except for the use of brief quotations in a book review.

*To the unsung heroes:
The brave mothers who inspire their daughters to
break free from stereotypes.*

CONTENTS

Before You Start	vii
Introduction	ix
1. Dick, Kerr Ladies — Pioneers Of Possibility	1
2. Nadia Nadim — The Goal-scoring Refugee Doctor	6
3. The Reggae Girlz — From Go Fund Me to Try And Get Past Me	9
4. Sam Kerr — Reluctant Hero of the Game	14
5. Ada Hegerberg — Ahead Of Her Time	18
6. Hidden Heroines of 1971 — The Forgotten World Cup	23
7. Linda Caicedo — One Year Three World Cups	27
8. Sandrine Dusang — French Fighter With No Frontiers	31
9. Debinha — Defeating Demons	34
10. Spain Ladies 2023 — Triumph Beyond The Trophy	39
11. The Lionesses — Roaring Triumph To Conquer Europe	43
12. Fara Williams — A Journey Of Resilience And Inspiration	47
13. Megan Rapinoe — Revolution And Triumph Beyond The Field	52
14. Monika Staab — Paving The Path In The Desert Kingdom	56
15. Khadija "Bunny" Shaw — A Journey Of Determination	60
16. Hope Powell — Powering Through The Glass Ceiling	65

17. Lily Parr — The Jewel In DKL's Crown	70
18. Mia Hamm — The Goal-getting Great	74
19. Alex Morgan — Striking for Change	78
20. Michelle Akers — True Giant Of The Game	82
21. Susan Whelan — The Genius Behind English Football's Greatest Triumph	86
22. Chan Yuen Ting — Showing Them How It's Done	91
23. Jacqui Oatley — Moulding The Perception Of Millions	95
24. Gurinder Chadha — Master Of The Mainstream	99
25. Karren Brady — The First Lady Of Football	102
26. Rebecca Welch — Whistling Her Way To The Top	105
27. Stéphanie Frappart — France's Fearless Pioneer	108
28. Eni Aluko — Unstoppable Spirit	112
29. Rebekah Stott —Tested Beyond Belief	117
30. Formiga — Formidable For Ages	121
31. Rafaelle Souza — Representing The Dreams Of Millions	125
32. Marta — Immortal	129
Afterword	135
Acknowledgments	137
About the Author	139

BEFORE YOU START

As you embark on this extraordinary journey through the history of women's football, please note that we may interchangeably use "soccer" to describe football—a different word for the same beautiful sport that unites us worldwide.

We have also designed the chapters to be read as stand-alone stories, so if you feel like doing so, jump straight into the chapter of your favourite heroine!

INTRODUCTION

In the heart of Lancashire in England, amidst the tumultuous era of the First World War, a group of resilient women ignited a spark. A spark so powerful that it would transcend the passage of time, fuelling and inspiring countless generations of young women after them.

This unique group of ladies laid the foundations for women's football's growth into the global movement it is today.

It is only fitting that we begin this book by paying tribute to the pioneers that were the Dick, Kerr Ladies.

CHAPTER 1
DICK, KERR LADIES — PIONEERS OF POSSIBILITY

As the First World War unfolded in 1914, the demand for ammunition in the UK skyrocketed. The Government turned to a company called Dick, Kerr & Co. to manufacture shells for the Armed Services. The entire factory transformed into a production hub, with women stepping in to fill the roles left vacant by men serving on the front lines. These women, known as munitionettes, became the hidden army on the home front, taking on every imaginable task to support Britain's war effort.

Amidst the gruelling work and dangerous conditions, women operated machinery, worked on the land, and took on roles in various industries. The munitionettes, exposed to toxic chemicals and hazardous environments, became one of the many unsung heroes of the war. Their sacrifices, often leading to health issues, showcased their unwavering commitment to supporting their country in its time of need.

During tea breaks and lunch, the munitions girls

found solace and camaraderie in friendly kickabouts with young male and female apprentices in this challenging landscape.

The turning point came in October 1917, after the men's football team had suffered a series of defeats to the women's team. That's when a young woman named Grace Sibbert had an innocuous idea.

Sibbert, a regular participant in the friendly games, proposed, "Come on, girls, let's give it a go. Let's form a ladies-only team. It'll be a laugh." The other women in the team accepted the challenge, and the Dick, Kerr Ladies (DKL) football team was born.

Things took an unexpected turn when the munitions factory was approached to raise money for wounded soldiers. It was suggested that they throw a charity concert, but the factory munitionettes proposed a charity football match instead.

Sibbert's innocuous idea was about to turn revolutionary.

On Christmas Day 1917, in front of 10,000 spectators, DKL played their first official match against the Arundel Coulthard Foundry Women's team. They won 4-0 and raised £600 for wounded soldiers (the equivalent of about $55,000 in today's money!).

Things went from strength to strength for the team. The 1920s marked the golden years for Dick, Kerr Ladies, with high-profile matches that captured the imagination of fans across the nation. A game against St Helens Ladies at Everton's Goodison Park, witnessed by 53,000 people, showcased the team's growing influence in the country's popular culture. That was followed by clashes at huge grounds like Manchester United's Old Trafford and Preston North End's Deepdale.

The Dick, Kerr Ladies were quickly turning women's football into a cultural phenomenon.

In 1920, they etched their names in history by playing the first international women's football game. Representing England, they faced off against a French team at Deepdale in front of 25,000 spectators, emerging victorious with a 2-0 win. This groundbreaking moment paved the way for the globalisation of women's football, proving that The Beautiful Game knew no gender boundaries.

This victory marked the beginning of an extraordinary journey for DKL. Their popularity skyrocketed, and their matches became major events, drawing crowds of almost 900,000 people in 1921 alone! The team played over sixty games that year, all while working full-time at the factory.

Storm clouds loomed, however, as The Football Association of England dealt a bitter blow. On 5 December 1921, The Football Association — known as FA for short — *banned* women's football and instructed all football clubs to refuse permission for ladies' matches to take place. This had a significant effect on ladies' football teams across the country. Despite the ban, DKL defied The FA and, against all odds, continued to play, showing that their resilience and grit were not restricted to the field of play.

The team's achievements during the 1920s and 1930s

were remarkable. The press lauded them as "World Champions," and they sailed to America to play a series of matches. Only when they got there did they realise the games were against men! Steadfast, they battled on and kept winning games, continuing to defy societal expectations of the time.

The Dick, Kerr Ladies, unfortunately, disbanded in 1965 due to a lack of players. It was the year before the men's English team won the World Cup, which could have seen a renewed interest in women's football. However, their legacy continued to have ripple effects in England and across the world. The Women's Football Association (WFA) was formed in 1969, and the ban imposed by The FA on women playing the sport was finally lifted in 1971, marking the beginning of a new era for women's football.

The long and arduous journey of women's football, from bans and restrictions to acceptance and global recognition, began because of the resilience and determination of the trailblazers that were the Dick, Kerr Ladies.

DKL wasn't just a football team but a symbol of cultural change. Their matches transcended the sport, becoming major events that challenged traditional gender roles. In an era of women fighting for recognition, they stood as beacons of empowerment, inspiring young women worldwide for many generations.

Their legacy lives on as an essential part of women's football history, a testament to their strength of character and toughness. They broke down barriers and changed attitudes towards women in sports, demonstrating that women could succeed in the field and beyond.

So, young women, lace up your boots with pride, knowing that the legacy of the Dick, Kerr Ladies lives on, inspiring everyone to believe in the power of their dreams and the resilience within themselves.

CHAPTER 2
NADIA NADIM — THE GOAL-SCORING REFUGEE DOCTOR

NADIA NADIM INSPIRES WITH EVERY ACTION SHE TAKES, whether on or off the football field. The Afghanistan-born Denmark international has led one of the most remarkable lives among the women featured in this book. Despite starting from a very disadvantaged position, she has shown the world that with determination, anything is possible.

Born in Afghanistan, Nadim's life took a tragic turn at a very early age when her father, a member of the Afghan army, was murdered by the Taliban. Left without a male figure in the family, Nadia and her sisters found themselves trapped at home. In a country where women's rights are limited, it would have been dangerous for her and her sisters to venture out of the house. Her mother used this time to homeschool her five daughters. Still, it wasn't long after the loss of their father that Nadim's courageous mother took them on another journey.

Armed with nothing but fake passports, Nadim's

mum placed her and her four sisters in the back of a truck, smuggling them out of Afghanistan into neighbouring Pakistan. From there, the family flew to Italy before embarking on another leg of their journey toward Scandinavia. They settled in a refugee camp in Randers, Denmark, where Nadia's life would slowly start to look up.

In the mornings, Nadim taught herself Danish, displaying the self-discipline and grit that would later define her career.

In the afternoons, through the fences of the refugee camp, she watched Danish girls playing football in a neighbouring field. It was a sight that sparked a love for the game from deep within her soul. For Nadim, coming from a country where women were heavily repressed, seeing girls play football was a complete revelation!

In the evenings, she honed her skills by playing with other refugee boys and girls, kicking a football around until it was too dark to see. When she felt ready, she gathered the courage to ask the girls across the fence if she could join them. They said yes, and from there, her football career took off!

Nadim went on to represent Denmark internationally, yet again overcoming obstacles — FIFA bureaucracy this time — to fulfil her dream of playing for her adopted country.

Her courage and determination served her well in football, leading her to win two top-flight leagues: One with the Portland Thorns in the USA and another with Paris St Germain in France, scoring over 200 goals in her professional career. Nadim inspired millions of young women to believe in their dreams.

But Nadim wanted to give back even more to society. She established a football foundation that helps underprivileged children in Denmark thrive through football. She has supported over 200 children who, like her, faced difficult upbringings as immigrants in new countries. In recognition of her efforts in promoting sports and gender equality, she was designated as a UNESCO Champion for Girls' and Women's Education in 2019.

Replicating her mother's dogged determination, Nadim balanced the physical demands of professional football with the mental challenges of pursuing a medical degree. In 2022, she qualified as a medical doctor, driven by her desire to help people beyond her football career.

"I want to be in a position where I can help people when I retire from the game," she said. "When I walk the corridors of the hospital in my white coat, I get this feeling I can do great things."

Indeed, Nadia Nadim has already achieved greatness, inspiring countless young women worldwide with her unwavering determination and relentless pursuit of her dreams. Her journey is a testament to the transformative power of resilience, proving that the impossible can be made possible with grit and a can-do attitude.

CHAPTER 3
THE REGGAE GIRLZ — FROM GO FUND ME TO TRY AND GET PAST ME

THIS IS THE TENACIOUS STORY OF THE REGGAE GIRLZ, OR, AS they are formally known, the Jamaican Women's National Football Team.

It's a story that carries the common thread of all the women in this book: a relentless, courageous fight to pursue their love for football – a love they showcased to the entire world at the 2023 World Cup in Australia and New Zealand.

Initially formed in 1991, The Reggae Girlz struggled from the start. Held back by lack of funding and support from the Jamaican Football Federation, they had no option but to disband in 2010. Despite being in the 21st century, the mentality within their own football federation would only see them last for 19 years.

But when the going gets tough, the tough get going. In 2014, four years after their initial setback, The Reggae Girlz rallied again to re-enter the international football scene and embarked on a mission to leave their mark on the global stage. The foundations of the original Reggae Girlz team were no longer in place, and their four-year absence from international football meant they had to start anew, facing significant challenges along the way.

By 2017, The Reggae Girlz had played so little competitive football that FIFA would not even give them a ranking — meaning they started their quest towards the 2019 World Cup unranked! Rather than deter them, this lack of recognition only intensified their determination to push themselves further, work harder, and strive for greater heights.

Defying the nay-sayers and overcoming the odds, The Reggae Girlz stunned the football world in France in 2019 when they became the first women from a Caribbean nation to qualify for the World Cup. Refusing to be deterred by the lack of support or their unranked status, they persisted in their quest. They demonstrated a resilience rarely seen before on a football pitch. Every day, they took to the field to showcase their talent and determination, proving their critics wrong when they earned their place among the world's elite teams.

Despite being knocked out in the group stages after conceding 12 goals, there were many positives to take. This should have been the springboard for future success in Jamaican women's football. After all, going from unranked to playing in a World Cup in a matter of months was a feat that no other country had done in the past!

However, life threw a curveball at The Reggae Girlz. The only people who didn't take notice of their 2019 success were, unfortunately, the people sitting at the helm of The Jamaican Football Federation.

Unimpressed and uninterested in their incredible achievements, the Jamaican football bosses showed no support for The Reggae Girlz. They were not being compensated, rewarded, or incentivised for their work on the field. Things got so bad that the daughter of the most famous Jamaican had to get involved.

Cedella Marley, daughter of Bob Marley, ramped up her efforts to get The Reggae Girlz the needed funding. It had been a battle she had been fighting against the Jamaican FA since their resurrection in 2014, but seeing The Reggae Girlz being pushed to the side *despite* their recent World Cup success was too much. Cedella Marley helped make the plight of the Reggae Girls a global issue.

On the field, unfazed by the lack of support from their Football Association, The Reggae Girlz went from strength to strength and qualified for the 2023 World Cup, held in Australia and New Zealand. Four years had passed since France 2019, and as the Jamaican women were progressing on the field, nothing was happening above them in the Jamaican Football Federation.

A month before the 2023 World Cup, support from the Jamaican Football Federation got so bad that Sandra Phillips-Brower, the mother of Jamaican midfielder Havana Solaun, set up a GoFundMe page to help pay for the costs that The Reggae Girlz were accumulating as they trained for the tournament. Her campaign helped raise more than $45,000!

Noticing the success of that GoFundMe page, The

Reggae Girlz Foundation set up another page. That also raised over $45,000—much-needed money that helped The Reggae Girlz with amenities such as training camps, staff support, travel, food, and match fees that the Jamaican Football Federation should have provided.

They say that darkness must be present for light to shine brightly. Being tested off the pitch in such extreme conditions was precisely the darkness that The Reggae Girlz needed to shine as brightly as they did in Australia and New Zealand.

Never in World Cup history has there been a better defensive display. In their first game, The Reggae Girlz faced the powerhouse that is France, and they didn't concede a single goal!

In their second game against Panama, they again showcased a defensive masterclass to keep a clean sheet. They won that game 1-0.

But it was against the greatest football nation in the world that they made their dent in the football universe. Brazil's women's football team, packed with the deadliest strikers and most skilful football players ever seen, came up against The Reggae Girlz. Having been fighting tooth and nail off the pitch, the Jamaicans showed the same fighting spirit on it. Brazil didn't have as much of a sniff at goal that day. The Reggae Girlz didn't concede against the Brazilians and knocked the football juggernauts out of the tournament! They went through the whole group stage without conceding a single goal!

They also became the first Caribbean nation (male or female) to advance to the second round of a World Cup, and they did it with the help of GoFundMe pages and Cedella Marley, *not* The Jamaican Football Federation, as expected. Never before had the World Cup seen such indomitable spirits, a resilience to fight for the most basic of human rights: equality. Rebecca Spencer, The Reggae Girlz goalkeeper, summed up this spirit nicely.

"When they don't believe in us - that just gives us more fire in our belly to go out there and do well."

Jamaica's World Cup journey sadly ended at the hands of Colombia in the next game - Catalina Usme scoring the solitary goal that The Reggae Girlz would concede in the campaign. The one that, sadly, cost them the tournament. However, what the Jamaican women's football team achieved that year was beyond measurable; they inspired millions of Caribbean girls from multiple countries to believe anything is possible. That success is possible *despite* the forces actively trying to stop you. All you need is self-belief and an unrelenting fighting spirit.

CHAPTER 4
SAM KERR — RELUCTANT HERO OF THE GAME

SAMANTHA KERR WAS BROUGHT UP PLAYING FOOTBALL FROM A very young age. Her dad and brother were professional football players, and every conversation in her household revolved around football.

You would be forgiven for thinking that, given her football-mad upbringing, she was destined to be a football star. But like many other women in this book, her story is one of resilience and determination to start afresh after being knocked down.

Why?

Because the football played and spoken about in her household was not *our* football, it was what the *Australians* call football. Also known as AFL, Aussie Rules, or just Footie, it is the national sport of Australia, and you can use your hands as well as your feet when playing it—it's very different from our football.

Following in the footsteps of her dad and brother, Samantha was kicking an AFL football from the moment she could walk. She began playing competitively at the age of 9 and continued until she was 12 years old. It wasn't until then that the boys on her team realised she was a girl. Their reaction was so extreme that some of them even started crying upon learning the truth about Sam's gender.

Around that time, the very physical game of Aussie Rules started hampering Sam's progress. Despite dominating through her AFL skills, the boys quickly outgrew and outmuscled her as they reached puberty. It seemed skill alone wouldn't see her thrive in the sport as a young woman growing up in Perth – mainly because there were no women's AFL teams she could join.

At 12, Samantha was forced to give up her dreams of playing professional AFL. Despite her dazzling ability with a ball, it was evident that the Aussie Rules world wasn't ready for a woman superstar yet. Reluctantly, Samantha Kerr tried her hand (or should we say feet?) at football instead of Aussie Rules.

Luckily for global football, AFL's loss was football's gain.

It wasn't an immediate gain. Sam was terrible at this new sport she was trying out. She was only 12, however —there was time to learn and improve, and Kerr, marked by a dogged determination to be the absolute best version of herself, decided to become as good at football as she was at AFL—a journey that only took a few months!

Denied the chance to play the sport she loved, she channeled her disappointment into a relentless drive to excel in her new passion. Kerr's transition from AFL to football was remarkable, and she quickly rose through the ranks, making her professional debut for club and country by the age of 15. Sam took to a new sport better than any athlete in the history of sport. It was a testament to her raw talent and unrelenting determination.

Kerr, perhaps knowing that she was only beginning her trajectory to greatness (or could it have been nerves?), asked her family *not* to watch her football debut for Australia!

Despite displaying a talent and skill that had never been seen in Australian football, the extent of the Perth attacker's abilities was yet to be revealed. The world was on the brink of witnessing one of the greatest football players ever emerge. For all her exceptional skills on the field, her remarkable journey to success was more a testament to her inner strength and resilience. She harnessed the disappointment and frustration of being subjected to a system that lagged behind societal progress, ultimately rising to become the best football player of her generation.

Many players might have considered their journey complete upon representing their country; after all, that is the pinnacle of anyone's career. However, this achievement only served as a springboard to further greatness for Kerr. It fuelled her determination to continue blazing new trails and cementing her place as one of the all-time greats.

Kerr's goalscoring record speaks for itself. She is the only player to be the top scorer in a season in the USA,

English, and Australian leagues! She is also the highest-scoring player for Australia's national team, eclipsing the record that male favourite Tim Cahill had up until 2022. Kerr is also only one of three women to have scored more than three goals in a World Cup—she achieved this by putting four goals past Jamaica in the 2019 World Cup.

Kerr's story is an excellent example of never giving up despite challenges. Imagine being surrounded by family members all sharing the same passion, only to have that passion taken away from you. Her journey is a testament to resilience and hope, demonstrating that there's always another route to success when one path closes.

Not only did she find success, but she also became arguably the most talented football player the world has ever seen, having been named a finalist for the FIFA Female Player of the Year three times! Samantha Kerr inspires millions of girls worldwide who are mesmerised by the quality of her goals and the backflip celebration accompanying them. Her love for the game and her country is infectious, and she continues to set records through her athletic prowess — most notably her ability to score headed goals despite her short stature.

So, if you ever feel like things aren't going your way, think of Sam Kerr's journey to football stardom. Who knows, with enough perseverance, you too can reach the pinnacle of success, just like she did!

CHAPTER 5
ADA HEGERBERG — AHEAD OF HER TIME

At the end of 2018, Ada Hegerberg picked up her prize for being the best football player on the planet. She lined up with her male peers Kylian Mbappe and Luka Modric to collect her award — her peers had only just come off the back of playing in a World Cup final. Hegerberg's award was remarkable because she was the best player on Earth, having *not* played for her national team for 18 months! And the reason why she gave up playing for her nation is what made her an inspiration to millions.

Hegerberg grew up in the small, scenic, sleepy town of Sunndalsøra in Norway. From a very early age, she lived and breathed football. Much like the Kerrs (Chapter 4), the sport they loved dominated most family conversations. Her father, mother, brother, *and* sister all played The Beautiful Game. It was inevitable that Ada would also play football, but what was unprecedented was the impact she would make on the sport, both on and off the field.

Ada's skills were honed by a father who frequently and rigorously trained with his children. With two older siblings to compete against, Ada quickly showcased an uncanny ability to receive a ball, turn on the spot, and shoot on target from a very early age. This desirable quality would ultimately pave the way for her to become one of the most lethal goal-scoring legends the women's game has ever seen.

Supported by parents who relentlessly encouraged her to strive for excellence, Ada made her mark in Norway's professional league by achieving a remarkable feat in her debut for Kolbotn FC: scoring three goals in just seven minutes.

Seven minutes. Three goals. On her professional debut!

Let that sink in.

This extraordinary accomplishment showed she was a force of nature destined for greatness. It wasn't long before Olympique Lyonnais of France picked her up – her prowess was now on show for the world to rejoice. For any doubters who would argue that her incredible debut for Kolbotn was because of a weaker league, she would go on to prove them wrong by scoring a hat-trick in 30 minutes of the 2019 Champions League Final! The pinnacle of Club Competitions and Ada was scoring goals for fun. This effortless nature was, no doubt, due to the countless hours her dad had invested in her training, but also the encouraging words of her mum, who had had a tougher time trying to become a professional football player herself.

By the time Ada scored a 30-minute hat-trick in the Champions League final against Barcelona, she was already officially recognised as the best player in the world. She would go on to win (at the time of writing) six Champions League trophies. In doing so, she became the Women's Champions League top scorer and reached her half-century of goals faster than any other player on Earth (male or female).

"You need to try and put as much quality across in everything that you do," she says, and there isn't a finisher of better quality in the women's game. Ada would go on to win the inaugural Women's Ballon d'Or, but not content with impressing us with her football skills, Ada delivered her acceptance speech in two languages, neither of which were her mother tongue. She also elegantly navigated the casual sexism thrown her way on stage when she received the award. Evidently, it wasn't just defenders on the pitch with whom she could easily glide past.

Her instinctive finishing and football prowess are reason enough to honour her with a chapter in this book – but the work she's done off the field elevates her status as one of the most incredible personalities in the world of sport.

She retired from playing for her country at the pinnacle of her career, at only 22 years of age. She did this in protest at the inequality between how the Norwegian Football Federation treated the male and female teams, and she did so at a time when she was averaging a goals-to-game ratio that bettered one a game!

Although Ada didn't like the term "boycott", she did not represent her country until gender inequality disappeared. In this fight, she sacrificed one of the most cherished opportunities professional football players receive from the world: participation in the 2019 World Cup.

Ada knew that sacrificing an appearance in the most important tournament of world football was worth it to empower women worldwide. While the world missed out on seeing the best player in the world at the 2019 World Cup, Ada was fighting for something bigger: equality in the sport in her native Norway. She had enough of women being paid less than their male counterparts, of training on inferior pitches, and of the carelessness given to the boots they played in — the little details that went unnoticed by many but that the Norwegian Football Federation wouldn't even dream of allowing to occur if it were the men's team.

As soon as she refused to play for Norway, the federation took notice and announced that the men's and women's national teams would be paid equally. They were wrong if they thought this would bring back the world's best player. Ada was fighting for something bigger than just money. She wanted equal treatment in all aspects of the game: advice, facilities, training, performance, and culture.

It would take the best player in the world five years of exile and a missed World Cup for her to return to international football. Her five years of activism showed the world that despite apparent progress in 21st-century women's football, the reality was far from ideal.

Ada's stance was unbreakable; she was determined to fight until Norway's female players were treated equally to their male counterparts. Despite facing battles and accusations of hijacking Norway's World Cup preparations, Hegerberg finally felt change was happening when Lise Klaveness was elected president of the Norwegian Football Federation. Having a woman in charge who shared the same vision as Hegerberg was the catalyst needed for her to return to the national team. It was vindication for Ada, showing the world that she could succeed in off-the-pitch battles too, paving the way for other women to be given the same opportunities in the future.

In her first game back, Hegerberg picked up right where she left off, scoring a hat-trick in a 5–1 win against Kosovo in a 2023 World Cup qualifier. She is now back playing for Norway, having fought and won one of her biggest battles. While there's no doubt that the international game was poorer for her absence, the strides Hegerberg made for women worldwide were immeasurable. Her contributions have paved the way for the future of the women's game and the dreams of millions of girls who will come after her, inspiring them to emulate her achievements, either on or off the field.

Unbeknownst to the world, Ada Hegerberg wasn't the first Scandinavian football superstar. In 1971, an extraordinary woman from Denmark made significant waves...

CHAPTER 6
HIDDEN HEROINES OF 1971 — THE FORGOTTEN WORLD CUP

"One simply forgets one's own history," said Susanne "Susy" Augustesen, one of only two female players to score a hat-trick in a World Cup final. She scored her three goals in front of a record crowd of over 110,000 screaming fans.

Unfortunately for the Danish striker, her remarkable achievement happened during an *unofficial* women's World Cup, leaving her name buried in the archives of football history for nearly half a century.

This unsanctioned World Cup came in 1971 in the same vibrant Mexican stadiums where Pelé had won the men's World Cup only a year earlier. This World Cup was more than a tournament — it had an air of change. A revolution was brewing, not of political upheaval, but of a sporting nature. The world was about to witness the birth of a phenomenon that would forever change the landscape of women's football, even if the tale slipped into the shadows of history for five long decades!

At a time when women's football was banned in many countries—even *illegal* in countries like Brazil—Mexican media giants Televisa were keen to capitalise on the commercial success they had just had by broadcasting the men's 1970 World Cup. They teamed up with Italian drinks manufacturer Rossi to host a women-only football tournament with six national teams from Latin America and Europe, including hosts Mexico, which qualified automatically.

In all but name, the tournament bore the hallmark of a World Cup. This groundbreaking event marked the second of its kind, following Rossi's successful hosting of a similar event in Italy the year prior. As the main sponsor, Rossi covered all expenses, from flights to kits, ensuring every participant was equipped for the occasion. However, the players embarking on this historic journey faced harsh criticism and condemnation from within their own football federations, labeled as "rebels," they were accused of neglecting their societal duties as women by daring to pursue a dream deemed unworthy by conventional standards.

These rebels weren't given the respect their trailblazing ways commanded. The organisers sadly marketed the tournament with a misogynistic attitude that was prevalent at the time—they advertised the tournament by promising the two things that men presumably loved: football and women. As if that wasn't enough, they also relied on cheap gimmicks like pink-hooped goalposts and pop-up hair and beauty salons outside the stadiums. They wanted to draw in the crowds, and that is precisely what they did.

The record crowds that watched these women battle it out in the summer heat of Mexico City and Guadalajara — the two host cities — had never been seen before! To this day, they stand as world-record crowds for female sport.

These paying spectators, often nearing the staggering one hundred thousand, filled the massive stadiums, eager to witness the fierce battles unfold on the pitch. And we *mean* battles.

Rossi and Televisa's aim was purely commercial gain, but the girls weren't there to make up the numbers. They were fierce competitors, driven by an unyielding determination to honour their countries' colours—a commitment evidenced by two English girls returning home in casts after their game against Argentina. Yet, the pinnacle of the fighting spirit and competitiveness came in the semi-final game between Mexico and Italy when the referee interfered with Italian midfielder Elena Schiavo's goal.

The 23-year-old midfielder scored a beauty of a rocket with her right foot, only for the referee to inexplicably rule it out. It was the second goal he had ruled out in favour of the host nation, and Schiavo lost her temper. A massive brawl erupted in the middle of the field. Players, managers, referees, and even bystanders had to get involved to calm things down. In that moment, it was abundantly clear: the women on the field were determined to emerge victorious at any cost.

Mexico progressed to the final, where they met a Danish side fresh from winning the previous "World Cup" only 12 months prior. Denmark also had Susanne Augustesen, a 15-year-old prodigy, who would single-handedly demolish the home crowd's hopes by scoring a hat-trick in the final. Despite breaking home crowd hearts, Augustesen would go on to lift the "World Cup" trophy in front of more than a hundred thousand people.

The girls of '71 arrived from their respective countries as outcasts, ostracised for their love of the sport, only to enter a parallel universe in Mexico that summer. They were embraced by a nation that loved the spectacle of sport—even if it had been orchestrated by a well-oiled marketing machine—and shattered the most deeply entrenched perceptions of the era.

At a time when globalisation of the sport was starting to take off because of TV cameras, they inspired a legion of girls to be fearless and chase their dreams. Their presence on the world stage showcased the untapped potential of a female tournament, challenging entrenched norms and paving the way for change. It wasn't long before Football Associations around the world lifted their bans. Their pioneering spirit and unwavering determination laid the foundation for FIFA to officially recognise and sanction these tournaments a few years later. They were true football pioneers whose history should never be forgotten.

CHAPTER 7
LINDA CAICEDO — ONE YEAR THREE WORLD CUPS

Linda Caicedo is one of the most remarkable girls in football. We use the term "girl" because she's barely completed her first year of adulthood at the time of writing. This girl achieved more in her teenage years than most women will achieve in their lifetime.

Growing up in Valle Del Cauca in Colombia, her dad asked her what she wanted as a present for her 5th birthday.

"Would you like a doll, sweetheart?" He asked.

"No, I want a football and boots," she responded.

She clearly loved football from a very early age.

In a country where football equality lags behind its European counterparts, Caicedo made waves and shattered stereotypes early on by becoming the first girl to break into the renowned Villagorgona football academy in Cali.

On the 15th of July 2019, at only 14 years of age, she made her stamp on Colombian football. This was when she debuted in the professional women's league with America de Cali. She came on as a substitute on 75 minutes, and 4 minutes later, she received the ball on the halfway line and set off on a run towards the opposing goal, leaving three defenders on the floor — it seemed futile and foolish to try and stop her. She then elegantly put the ball in the back of the net to score her first senior goal. Linda Caicedo had announced herself well on the football scene. A few months later, still only 14 but having just become Colombian champion, there was no stopping her. Or was there?

In the months following her remarkable breakthrough on the Colombian football scene, Caicedo began experiencing stomach pain. Initially misdiagnosed as gastritis by doctors, it wasn't until Caicedo persisted in complaining about the pain that they discovered a cancerous tumour in her abdomen.

Caicedo was diagnosed with ovarian cancer. It appeared that if defenders couldn't stop her on the field, cancer might thwart her off it.

Having just turned 15, Caicedo put her body through multiple treatments and surgeries, something that made her think she would never play professionally again. She battled physically as well as mentally, and after a few months, she was given the all-clear by doctors. Caicedo had beaten cancer, and she was ready to take on the world. And take on the world she did.

She moved from America de Cali to city rivals Deportivo Cali and won another Colombian championship. While many professionals play for a lifetime without winning a single title, Caicedo, at only 15, had already beaten cancer and won *two* national championships in her native country!

During the 2022-2023 season, Caicedo had the most remarkable season any male or female football player could ever have. This period saw her status skyrocket into that of a global phenomenon.

In September, she represented Colombia in the U20s World Cup in Costa Rica. Two months later, she played in the U17 World Cup in India.

Caicedo shone brightly during the U17 World Cup, contributing significantly to Colombia's journey to the final, although they ultimately lost to Spain. However, there was a silver lining for Caicedo in that defeat; her performance caught the eye of Spanish scouts, and a few months later, Real Madrid, the world's biggest club, signed her. Real Madrid recognised Caicedo's talent and secured her services immediately.

As if participating in two World Cups in two months wasn't enough, Caicedo went on to represent Colombia at the 2023 World Cup held in Australia and New Zealand. No player has ever played in three World Cups in 12 months, and it's a feat that will likely never happen again.

The meteoric rise of Caicedo inspires women worldwide, particularly in her native Colombia. Her achievements are remarkable not only because she overcame cancer at a young age but also because she did so in a country where machismo culture still prevails. Despite the challenges, she rose to prominence with style and grace, breaking barriers and defying stereotypes.

Her superb winning goal against Germany in the 2023 World Cup provided one of the biggest upsets in the history of the women's game. Unfortunately for Caicedo and Colombia, England knocked them out. Still, at the very tender age of 18, Caicedo had already left an indelible mark on world football and countless girls worldwide.

There is no doubt that Caicedo will become a global superstar. Still, it is a testament to her skill, determination, and strength of character that, at only 18 and having already signed for the biggest club, we can *already* talk about her as a legend of the game.

It is unlikely that any other player will ever win the U17 World Cup's second-best player award, the U20 World Cup's Golden Ball, and help knock out Juggernauts Germany out of a World Cup—all in 12 months!

In the words of a famous saying, "Shoot for the moon. Even if you miss, you'll land among the stars." For any young woman aspiring to a professional football career, aiming to emulate Caicedo's remarkable journey is akin to shooting for the moon. Even if you fall short, you'll still achieve greatness in football.

CHAPTER 8
SANDRINE DUSANG — FRENCH FIGHTER WITH NO FRONTIERS

MUCH LIKE NADIA NADIM'S (CHAPTER 2) STORY, SANDRINE Dusang's tale begins by following in the footsteps of the determined woman who was her mother.

Seeing that her young daughter much-preferred football training to dance lessons, Dusang's mother consistently gave up her precious time three times a week to drive Sandrine on a two-hour return journey to the nearest town with a girls' football team.

Dusang's mother's perseverance paid off for her daughter and, in time and unbeknownst to her, for tens of thousands of other women across France.

Sandrine Dusang rose through the ranks at her club, Olympique Lyonnais. She established herself as a hard-tackling central defender who took no prisoners. While ruthless on the pitch, she noticed a stark contrast between herself and her male counterparts at Olympique Lyonnais. Unlike them, she had to balance her football career with a job in the club's marketing department.

She often rushed from her 9-5 office job to barely make it in time for training. This was despite being a French international representing her country at the 2005 European Championships!

The balance had to change within her club's male/female teams. Thus, showing the same tenacity and perseverance as she did in the centre of the defence, she took on the challenge of changing how professional female football players were treated in France.

It wasn't until years of rallying influential people in the sport, and together with other prominent football players like Corinne Diacre and Laura Georges, that she was finally able to make one of her most significant dents in French football. Together with other French female football players, she made professional football clubs offer female players contracts *instead* of token match fees, which were common practice at the time and often amounted to meagre amounts.

Even after retiring from the national side, her relentless pressure on the authorities to change the status quo continued to shine through. She hung up her boots but not her passion for advocating women's rights, striving to make football a more inclusive game. Her advocacy for equal opportunities in the sport was evident by her role in editing the leading French news site Foot d'Elles ("Women's Football"), which promotes women's football and diversity in sport.

In her pursuit to fight against inequality, and showing the same relentless drive that had secured French female players contracts, she went one step further than any female football player ever had on the small island of Corsica. When she arrived at the Mediterranean island to play, she immediately noticed that female Corsican teams were only allowed to play in regional competitions and not against teams from mainland France. If male teams based in other continents like French Guiana could play in domestic cup competitions in mainland France, she saw no reason why Corsican women, from an island just off the country, couldn't be represented in the women's French domestic cup.

Dusang once again blazed a trail, setting new precedents along the way, and had the incredible outcome of smashing a few more glass ceilings. Her work and perseverance in lobbying Corsican politicians led to countless Corsican women showcasing their football skills on the mainland of France by playing for the first time in the Coupe de France competition in December 2022.

Dusang stands alone in French football as a bastion of hope for a more equal playing field. Her fierce determination and persistent drive to blaze new trails will monumentally impact countless future generations of French female football players. She ignited a spark that will undoubtedly become a blaze to burn for years to come.

CHAPTER 9
DEBINHA — DEFEATING DEMONS

BRAZILIAN FOOTBALL PLAYERS ARE OFTEN DEFINED BY TWO MAIN narratives: a tough upbringing in poverty-stricken towns and an awe-inspiring flair when showcasing their talent on the football field.

Brazilian superstar Debinha is no exception—she's an absolute joy to watch on the field. Yet, in a country where most football players face significant challenges during childhood, her exceptionally tough upbringing makes her journey into football even more remarkable.

Debinha's love for football was inspired by the Brasopolis neighbourhood she grew up in. Whenever the national team played, the neighbours would go wild for the games, and together with her sisters Katia and Rubiana, Debinha would eagerly gather around the big screens in the main square to watch the Seleção play — their community would come alive with enthusiasm and excitement.

But amidst the cheers and celebrations, Debinha's

journey was marked by challenges and adversity. As a young girl with a passion for football, she faced ridicule and bullying from an early age. The boys, perhaps concerned at being outplayed by a girl, would tease her, and the girls, who couldn't understand her love for the sport, would joke about the sporty clothes she'd often wear.

Even her mother, concerned for her daughter's well-being, urged her to conform to societal expectations and abandon her dreams of playing with the boys. Her mum often told her to dress more femininely or tie her hair tighter to fit in more easily.

Yet, at a very early age, Debinha refused to be swayed by the doubts and criticisms surrounding her. She embraced her love for football with tireless resolve, finding joy and freedom on the pitch where she could express her true self.

There was one person who understood her love for the sport, and that was her father. Unfortunately, he struggled with alcoholism, often being absent-minded at home and unable to connect with the family in a meaningful way. This was very much to Debinha's disappointment.

Her dad's struggle with alcoholism cast a shadow over the family's lives. Debinha couldn't comprehend why he couldn't simply stop drinking, why he couldn't see the pain it caused his wife and daughters. However, amidst the darkness, there were moments of light; when her father was sober, he encouraged his daughter's passion for football. He even persuaded Debinha's mother to support her dream of becoming a professional football player.

At 14, Debinha got accepted to play for one of Brazil's most prominent teams, Santos. The same club that Pelé — the world's greatest male player — had played for!

Her mum's reluctance to allow her to play professionally kept Debinha in Brasopolis — Santos was apparently too far away. Her mum, perhaps out of love for her daughter, chose to keep her daughter close to her. It could have spelled the end of a promising career.

At 16, Debinha was presented with another opportunity to play for one of Brazil's most prominent teams, and this time, she took it, packing her bag and heading to Saad Esporte Clube. It must have been tough for Debinha to go against her mother's wishes, but she knew that playing football was her destiny!

There was just one obstacle, however. Debinha needed her mother's signature on Saad's release form to play for the club. So she went to the factory where her mother worked and begged and cried for hours for her signature. Her mother, grappling with her own demons, cried too, as she didn't want her daughter to leave. Eventually, she agreed to sign.

Debinha was relentless in pursuing her dream of becoming a professional football player. The tears shed at the factory gate as she departed for Saad were a poignant reminder of her family's sacrifices to support her aspirations. Unbeknownst to Debinha at the time, this departure marked the beginning of a bout of depression for her mother. Upon learning about her mother's condition, Debinha became even more determined to succeed as a professional football player.

The journey was the start of a promising path that took her far from the familiar streets of Brazil and to the distant land of Korea, where homesickness and longing weighed heavily on her heart. Despite the allure of a promising opportunity in Seoul, Debinha couldn't shake the feeling of displacement and loneliness that engulfed her in a foreign land. She came back to Brazil after only ten days.

Her short time abroad was a testament to her determination to make it big. It was a period marked by struggles and challenges that tested her resolve. Yet, amidst the uncertainty and doubt, Debinha firmly believed that football was on her pathway, simply not in Korea.

After a short stint in Brazil, she had another international opportunity in Norway. This was slightly different from Korea, as she found other Brazilians to acclimate to foreign lands with.

Within months, Debinha got a call for Brazil's national team—it was a dream come true! It was a moment of validation for years of hard work and dedication. Playing alongside legends like Formiga (Chapter 30) and Marta (Chapter 32)—the same women she had watched on TV all those years earlier—filled her with a sense of pride and purpose as she represented her country on the world stage.

When she told her mum about the call-up, tears streamed down their faces again, but this time, they were tears of joy and pride. That's when they knew that all their sacrifices had paid off.

Both Debinha's parents fought off their collective demons (alcoholism and depression) and now follow their daughter fervently on football pitches across the world.

Today, as a professional athlete with the North Carolina Courage and with more than 140 appearances for the Brazilian national team, Debinha continues to chase her dreams with unwavering determination. Every match is an opportunity for her to honour her family, pave the way for women who want to pursue a career in football, and inspire the next generation of Brazilian girls to believe in themselves and pursue their passions fearlessly.

Her journey is a testament to the strength of the human spirit and the power of perseverance. She attributes this perseverance to her family, but her unwavering belief in the possibility of achieving anything through hard work and dedication drives her work ethic. This ethos is best captured by the words she tattooed on her leg: "WHEN I THINK I'VE REACHED MY LIMIT, I FIND THAT I HAVE THE STRENGTH TO GO BEYOND..."

Wise words that will inspire *anyone* looking to reach their goals.

CHAPTER 10
SPAIN LADIES 2023 — TRIUMPH BEYOND THE TROPHY

On a chilly Sydney evening in August 2023, Spain triumphed over England in the World Cup final.

A single goal by Olga Carmona proved decisive in the fiercely contested match against the reigning European champions. The significance of Spain's victory against such formidable opponents couldn't be overstated.

However, these women's monumental impact extended far beyond the football pitch. Their transformation journey began long before the final whistle, with a bold stand for change on and off the field.

Months before the tournament, 15 of the top players of the Spanish national team united to demand improved working conditions from the Spanish Football Association. They sought better support to safeguard their mental and physical well-being and advocated for professional treatment befitting elite athletes. Hailing from prestigious clubs like Barcelona and Manchester

City, these players knew firsthand the standards required for peak performance.

Yet, their plea was met with resistance from a predominantly male Football Association entrenched in a macho culture. The male manager of the women's team received the support of the president of the Football Association. In contrast, 12 of the 15 women who requested change were banned in retaliation for their demands!

Undeterred by patriarchal obstacles, a weakened Spanish team ventured to Australia and New Zealand for the 2023 World Cup — they were determined to make their mark. Despite the absence of key players, they presented a united front, refusing to be marginalised or silenced. They were there to do their job — and what a job they did!

Their resilience and determination shone through as they showcased their exceptional talent and skill on the world stage. They proved to be a well-drilled team, and with every goal scored and victory celebrated, they asserted their dominance and proved themselves worthy of the title. In a thrilling finale with England, and having missed a penalty during the game, they emerged victorious! Apart from a blip with Japan, they had beaten every team in front of them during the tournament. After seven hard-fought matches, they were the undisputed world champions!

While the celebrations should have marked the end of their journey, a troubling incident during the victory ceremony cast a shadow over their triumph. In front of a global audience, the president of the Spanish Football Association crossed a line by kissing Jenni Hermoso without her consent.

The incident sparked widespread outrage and ignited a powerful movement, with players and supporters rallying behind Jenni and condemning the president's actions. It served as a stark reminder of the ongoing battle against toxic masculinity and the urgent need for gender equality in sports.

Jenni and her teammates had already been fighting for fair treatment and support from the Football Federation before the tournament. Their demands for respect and equality were resolute, even in adversity. The president's actions underscored the entrenched misogyny within the Spanish football hierarchy, further fuelling the girls' determination to drive change.

Buoyed by global support, Jenni stood firm against coercive attempts from the Spanish Football Association to silence her. Together with her teammates, their unwavering resolve shattered the systemic male chauvinism that had long plagued Spanish football. In a remarkable turn of events, the federation's president and the women's team manager resigned after the scandal.

At the time of writing, the former president will face trial for his misconduct. Hermoso's courage has set a precedent for future generations to come — inspiring young girls to stand up and challenge societal norms.

The Spain Ladies of 2023 epitomise the spirit of resilience and empowerment, demonstrating that women's football is not just about goals and trophies but about breaking barriers and shaping a more inclusive future. And while there is still a long way to go in their battle for equality, they ignited Spain's own #metoo movement, leaving an indelible mark on the world of sports and paving the way for a brighter, more equitable future.

CHAPTER II
THE LIONESSES — ROARING TRIUMPH TO CONQUER EUROPE

Suppose one ever finds themselves short of superlatives to describe Spain's remarkable World Cup victory in 2023. In that case, it's worth remembering what their World Cup final rivals, England, had achieved just 12 months prior.

In women's football, few victories shine as brightly as the historic triumph of England's Lionesses at Euro 2022. Their remarkable journey to glory ended a 56-year wait for a major tournament victory. It sparked a lasting wave of inspiration across the country.

Let's delve into the remarkable tale of how the Lionesses defied the odds, transformed the landscape of football in England, and captured the hearts of a nation.

As we saw in Chapter 1, the roots of women's football in England run deep, with pioneers like the Dick, Kerr Ladies during World War I laying the groundwork for future generations. However, progress was hampered by decades of underinvestment, discrimination, and a close-to 50-year ban on women's football from FA-affiliated clubs and grounds.

Despite these challenges, the seeds of change sown by the Dick, Kerr Ladies continued to grow. These seeds were watered by the resilience and determination of many passionate women after them.

In 2017, The FA unveiled a "gameplan for growth," signalling a new era of commitment to women's football development. Apologies for past injustices were coupled with ambitious targets, including winning a major tournament by the 2021 Euros (which, due to Covid, was played in 2022) or the 2023 World Cup. The puzzle pieces were meticulously crafted, with the arrival of Dutch manager Sarina Wiegman serving as the final stroke of genius from The FA. Wiegman's leadership and strategic vision infused the team with belief and purpose, setting the stage for a historic triumph.

The Lionesses' Euro 2022 journey was not without its challenges. Mid-tournament Covid absences threatened to derail their momentum, while other players faced significant injury setbacks. Yet, amidst the pressure to succeed on home soil, the Lionesses stood tall, fuelled by a collective will to rewrite history. A determined Leah Williamson led their journey to the final, her unfaltering focus showcasing the true spirit of champions.

As the Lionesses advanced to the final, the nation rallied behind them with tireless support. Their dominance on the field captured the imagination of fans across England, igniting a fervour of excitement and anticipation not seen since the European Championships of 1996. With each victory, the roar of the Lionesses grew louder. Bronze, Williamson, Kelly & Co mesmerised a nation that had fallen out of love with international football for decades. The country well and truly got a case of fever: European Championship Fever.

They not only showed a self-deprecating country what it was like to dream big, but also inspired their fellow countrymen and women to proudly declare themselves English! The sentiment echoed through stadiums and streets alike. The final showdown was not just a game; it was a historic moment poised to redefine the landscape of football in England. And it was a Chloe Kelly strike in the 110th minute, in front of nearly 90,000 fans at Wembley, that secured the legacy of the most impressive women's football team the United Kingdom has ever seen.

The Lionesses beat Germany 2-1 in the final game at Euro 2022 and, in doing so, marked a watershed moment in the history of women's football in England. Their success exceeded the boundaries of sport, inspiring a new generation of young girls to dream big and pursue their passions with untiring determination. What the Dick, Kerr Ladies had begun a hundred years earlier, this crop of young Lionesses was now refining for the next generation of English girls.

Beyond the accolades and celebrations, the Lionesses remained steadfast in their commitment to grow the game for women and ensure equal access for all. Their message resonated across communities, advocating for inclusivity, diversity, and empowerment.

Etching their names in glory, The Lionesses illuminated a path of inspiration for young women to follow. In a nation grappling with a cost-of-living crisis and inflation, they brought unity to a country in disarray. Despite the challenges, the Lionesses offered everyone in the country a brief period of hope, respite, and joy.

Never again would women's football be seen as anything but equal to their male counterparts. It marked a seismic change in English societal thinking, a testament to the grit, passion, and determination those girls showed for England that summer.

CHAPTER 12
FARA WILLIAMS — A JOURNEY OF RESILIENCE AND INSPIRATION

AFTER ENGLAND'S VICTORY IN THE 2022 EUROPEAN CUP final, a group of triumphant players rushed towards a figure standing on the sidelines — a former England player and an esteemed friend.

She had retired just the year before, but her influence on the team's journey to victory resonated deeply with her teammates. Chloe Kelly, the game's heroine with her winning goal against Germany, leapt into her arms, hugging her tightly. Lucy Bronze and Jill Scott followed suit, their jubilant embrace knocking this former player to the turf in a joyous heap.

Her name? Fara Williams.

The players rushing to Williams after securing the most significant victory of their careers encapsulated not just Fara Williams's sheer magnetism but also the profound impact she had on women's football in England.

Her story is of grit and resilience personified. It is a

story of chasing your dreams with every fibre of your being—regardless of the obstacles that life may throw at you. Obstacles that, in Fara's case, would derail the majority of people in her position. However, the way Williams tackled them serves as a dose of inspiration for aspiring athletes worldwide.

Fara's journey began on the unforgiving concrete pitches of Battersea, South London, where, driven by an insatiable — some would say even irrational — love for the game, she honed her skills alongside boys. Money was hard for Fara's family to come by; they struggled financially, threatening to crush her dreams early on. Fara's dedication, however, earned her a place in Chelsea's under-14 team at the tender age of 12.

It was the beginning of a journey fraught with challenges beyond the pitch. At 17, Williams's mother invited her aunt to live with them. Williams clashed so much with her aunt that she left the family home. She had nowhere to go and found herself living on the streets.

Fara's spirit remained unbroken. By day, she was achieving extraordinary feats on the football field, showcasing her talent and determination with each match she played for Charlton Athletic. But as the sun set and the lights at The Valley stadium in South East London dimmed, Fara's reality was starkly different. She found herself without a stable home, navigating the complexities of accommodation by staying in hostels or temporary shelters.

While living in these hostels, she would go on to make her England debut!

While people in the shelters were falling like dominoes to the temptations of drugs and alcohol, Williams was knuckling down to practice football. One of Fara's tactics to stay focused on her football while living in shared accommodation was to act as if she was suffering from mental health problems. She did this so that people wouldn't approach her or, even worse, harm her.

In the face of such adversity, Fara's passion for the game burned brighter than ever. Football became her refuge, a sanctuary where she could channel her energy and talent amidst the uncertainty of her circumstances. Her dedication and resilience on the pitch were matched only by her strength and perseverance off it, as she refused to let homelessness define her.

During her football journey, Fara met a lady called Hope Powell (more on her in Chapter 16), and she went on to become Fara's manager for over a decade.

Powell recognised Fara's potential as a player and person and offered her unwavering support, providing Fara with food when she was hungry and a sleeping bag when she had nowhere to sleep. She also encouraged her to study the tactical side of the game further to complement her athletic prowess on the field. It was under Powell's advice that Fara would go on to take her coaching badges. It was a move that Powell told her would provide a long-term future for her in the game.

Fara's journey from homelessness to international stardom is a testament to Hope Powell's transformative power of mentorship and compassion. She is a beautiful example of women supporting women.

However, after her move to Everton, Fara's career took a turn for the better under the watchful eye of her new manager, Mo Marley. At Everton, she flourished both on and off the pitch.

Affectionately known as "Queen Fara" by fans, she played a pivotal role in the club's success, winning titles and accolades that solidified her status as one of England's greatest players. Her contributions extended beyond the game itself, as she embraced her role as a community coach, inspiring the next generation of football players through her passion and dedication.

Fara's impact reverberated throughout the international stage, where she earned a record 172 appearances for England over nearly two decades.

From humble beginnings and unthinkable setbacks, she orchestrated grand spectacles witnessed by thousands at iconic venues like Wembley Stadium.

Fara Williams's journey is a testament to the power of perseverance, resilience, and steadfast belief in oneself. Women everywhere can draw inspiration from her story, finding strength in knowing that no amount of adversity can derail their hopes and dreams. She was instrumental in reshaping the landscape of women's football too, inspiring millions of girls to play The Beautiful Game and deepening the pool of talent that England will count on for years to come.

While she may not have lifted a major trophy, and as we saw from the Euro 2022 champions, her influence transcended mere victories. Her legacy is her indelible mark on the sport and the countless lives she touched along the way.

So, while Fara Williams wasn't on the pitch when England won Euro 2022, she was most definitely seen and felt in the heart of Wembley Stadium that evening. Amidst the jubilant celebrations of victory, Fara Williams stood as a beacon of inspiration for the generation who had just claimed European glory. Undoubtedly, through her newfound role in TV punditry, she inspired many generations of athletes yet to come.

CHAPTER 13
MEGAN RAPINOE — REVOLUTION AND TRIUMPH BEYOND THE FIELD

IN THE WORLD OF WOMEN'S FOOTBALL, FEW NAMES SHINE AS brightly as Megan Rapinoe's. A Symbol of encouragement for young women across the USA, she relentlessly pursued justice.

At 38, Megan Rapinoe bid farewell to a football career spanning 17 years and 63 days, leaving an indelible mark on the U.S. Women's National Team (USWNT). Playing in four women's World Cups, winning two, and contributing to the 2012 Olympic gold-winning squad, Rapinoe's on-field excellence is nothing short of legendary.

She scored 63 international goals, securing her place in history as the 10th-highest goal-scorer in USWNT history, and her 73 assists tie with the iconic Abby Wambach. However, Rapinoe's impact transcends statistics; it's a story of triumphs, challenges, and determination on and off the football field.

Rapinoe's ascent to stardom took a decisive turn

during the 2011 World Cup quarter-final against Brazil. A perfectly executed long pass to Abby Wambach allowed the forward to head the goal that got the U.S. a late equaliser against the Brazilians. The game went to penalty kicks, culminating in a victory for the USA. That Wambach goal was voted the best goal in the history of women's World Cups, and the assist etched Rapinoe's name in football history, igniting a fire that would fuel her remarkable career.

Megan Rapinoe's influence extends far beyond her accomplishments in football, though. In 2016, she became the first white athlete to kneel during the national anthem, aligning herself with Colin Kaepernick's protest against police violence toward black people. Despite criticism, Rapinoe stood firm in her convictions, illustrating the power of using one's platform for social change.

"Being a gay American, I know what it means to look at the flag and not have it protect all of your liberties," she declared. Rapinoe emphasised the importance of solidarity and support across racial lines through her actions.

While everyone knew of her talent *on* the field, by the time the 2019 women's World Cup in France came around, it highlighted Rapinoe's unyielding advocacy *off* it. In public boldness, she stood up to the person often dubbed 'the most powerful man in the world' and engaged in a public exchange with then-President Donald Trump. She stood tall against patriarchy and inequality. It was a battle that she easily won.

Back on the field in France, she won the Golden Boot for most goals scored in the tournament, many of which were celebrated with her iconic arms-outstretched pose. Rapinoe quickly became a hero to many that summer, but above all, a symbol of resistance and hope.

Rapinoe was a star player and a leader in the fight for gender equality. Alongside her USWNT teammates, she battled U.S. Soccer to rectify the pay disparities between the men's and women's teams. Their persistence led to a landmark victory in 2022, with a new contract for female players and a settlement that included $22 million in back pay. Rapinoe's dedication paved the way for a more equitable future in the women's game and gender equality in many other sports.

As an openly gay athlete, Rapinoe has become an LGBTQ+ icon and advocate. Her visibility helped break down barriers and challenge stereotypes, showing young women that authenticity is a source of strength. Rapinoe's relationship with her partner, WNBA star Sue Bird, exemplifies the power of love and support in navigating life's challenges.

In 2022, Megan Rapinoe received the Presidential Medal of Freedom from President Joe Biden, becoming the first football player and one of only six female athletes to receive this prestigious award. Biden acknowledged Rapinoe's championing the "essential American truth" that everyone deserves dignity and respect.

After hanging up her boots, her commitment to creating positive change remained steadfast. Teaming up with Sue Bird, she launched a production company to amplify underrepresented voices. While football will always be a part of her legacy, Rapinoe envisions a future where she owns a professional women's football team and continues her activism.

In her final on-field speech, Rapinoe expressed her gratitude to fans worldwide, acknowledging the growth she's experienced through their encouragement. She emphasised that the USWNT embodies the diverse spirit of the nation and called on fans to rally behind them as their greatest supporters.

Reflecting on the game's evolution since her debut, Rapinoe highlighted the power of selflessness and the broader impact of their fight for equality, "we've done that for other people," she shared, underlining the significance of representation and the profound changes witnessed throughout her career.

Megan Rapinoe is an inspiration, especially for young women in the USA. Rapinoe spent her career demonstrating the transformative potential of sports, showing resilience in the face of challenges, and leveraging her platform to champion equality and justice — even when she had to stand up to the biggest bullies! As she embarks on the next chapter of her life, Rapinoe leaves a legacy beyond the football field, empowering a new generation to dream boldly and fight for their beliefs!

CHAPTER 14
MONIKA STAAB — PAVING THE PATH IN THE DESERT KINGDOM

In the vast desert expanse of Saudi Arabia, where golden dunes stretch as far as the eye can see, a trailblazer named Monika Staab etches a path for young girls with dreams as boundless as the horizon. Appointed as the inaugural coach of the Saudi women's football team in August 2021, Staab embodies a fighting spirit from which young women worldwide can draw inspiration.

Growing up in the 1960s near Frankfurt in Germany, Staab faced a world where the idea of girls playing football was deemed unconventional, if not forbidden. A self-proclaimed tomboy, she defied societal norms, engaging in street football with boys from age four. In an era where girls' teams were nonexistent, Staab's journey into the world of football was a battle against the status quo.

At 11, against all odds, she secured a spot on an adult women's team. The commitment required to pursue her passion was nothing short of extraordinary. "We couldn't get a pitch until 9.30 pm. I wouldn't get home until 11 pm, and the next morning, I'd go to work at 5 am at my parents' bakery. Then I'd go to school at 7 am," reminisces Staab. This relentless pursuit of her dreams — juggling football, work, and education — laid the foundation for the indomitable spirit that defines her legacy.

Staab's journey took her beyond the borders of her homeland. At 18, she courageously moved to London to play for Queens Park Rangers. The challenges were immense — players weren't paid by the club and even had to pay to use the pitch. Despite these obstacles, Staab persisted and supported herself by cleaning hotel rooms. Her football odyssey continued with stints at Southampton and Paris Saint-Germain before she returned to Germany in 1984.

In her homeland, Staab faced not only the absence of payment for female players but also endured sexist comments from male counterparts. The road to acceptance for women in football was arduous, especially in the 20th century, but Staab's resilience never wavered. She kept playing football professionally until 1992 when women's football was still a sport very much marginalised in her home country. The turning point came in 2003 when Germany won the Women's World Cup, signalling a shift in attitudes towards women's football.

Staab is best known for her impact on football *after* retiring from playing the sport. As the manager of Eintracht Frankfurt, Staab played a pivotal role in the team's success. While in charge of the German team, she won countless cups, championships, and European trophies.

In 2007, she embarked on a global mission to develop women's football and enhance women's lives. Staab reached 86 countries, touching the lives of communities far and wide. In The Gambia, girls returned to the classroom through football. In Cambodia, victims of human trafficking found solace on the pitch.

To Staab, football is more than a game; it is a vehicle for empowerment. "Football is more than a game. It teaches you respect, tolerance, fair play, communication, and how to work as a team," she passionately declares. This belief led her to Saudi Arabia in 2020 when the Saudi Arabian Football Federation (SAFF) invited her to run the first professional coaching course for women. Nine months later, she stood at the helm of the newly formed national team.

Enthusiasm for women's football surged in Saudi Arabia, especially after the creation of the women's football department in 2019, allowing women to play professionally. Staab witnessed a transformation, with men and women attending matches together and girls gaining the right to play sports in schools. In a country where women's rights are severely restricted, Staab has been instrumental in eradicating dated beliefs and modernising the game. Two women's domestic leagues involving 25 clubs now thrive, marking a seismic shift in the kingdom's sports landscape.

Staab's leadership led the national team to four wins and two draws in their first seven international matches.

In February of the following year, she was promoted to national technical director, overseeing the continuous development of women's football in the kingdom. "I am here for women's football. These girls deserve to play the game as much as men do." Staab's focus on the game and empowering young women through football speaks volumes about her dedication to breaking barriers and creating opportunities. And she has chosen to do this in one of the most complicated countries to do it in.

In the scorching heat of Riyadh, where training temperatures reach 40 degrees, Staab continues to inspire and lead. As young girls in Saudi Arabia lace up their boots, they do so with the knowledge that a trailblazer named Monika Staab paved the way for their dreams to flourish in the desert kingdom. Through her story, Staab encourages young girls worldwide to embrace their passions, challenge norms, and, above all, believe in the power of their dreams.

CHAPTER 15
KHADIJA "BUNNY" SHAW — A JOURNEY OF DETERMINATION

On January 31st, 1997, a young girl named Khadija Shaw was born in the Jamaican city of Spanish Town. She was about to embark on a journey that would not only change her life but also serve as a guiding light for many girls across the world.

As the youngest of 13 children, Khadija Shaw's early years were marked by the lively atmosphere of a bustling household. Her parents, a shoemaker father and a poultry farmer mother, instilled the values of education in their children. However, Khadija's heart beat to a different rhythm—the rhythm of football echoing through the streets of her Caribbean island.

Khadija's nickname "Bunny" came from one of her older brothers, who playfully observed her affection for carrots. Bunny found her passion for football by watching her brother's matches on the dusty streets outside their home. The spectacle of neighbours gathering to bet on the outcome fascinated her, igniting a fire that demanded participation.

Initially hesitant about letting a girl into their game, the boys started Bunny off in the position that traditionally no one wants to fill: goalkeeper. However, that role taught her resilience, and she challenged stereotypes with every save she made.

Bunny's parents were not pleased with her newfound passion. The dream of becoming a professional football player clashed with their vision of academic success. Bunny's parents, valuing education above all else, couldn't fathom their daughter spending valuable time chasing a ball.

Undeterred, Bunny seized every opportunity to play, often negotiating with her mother for a chance to hit the streets. Dishwashing became a bargaining chip. She would offer to do the dishes after dinner, and in exchange, her mother would let her out on the streets to gain minutes playing football. As her football skills developed, so did her dream, a dream inspired by a World Cup poster adorning her bedroom wall.

Bunny faced an uphill battle in a country where organised women's football was virtually nonexistent. But destiny had plans for her. At 14, she earned a spot on the Jamaica Under 15s team, a moment that convinced her father of the potential of his daughter's passion. Swayed by the belief that it could be a valuable experience, Bunny's indecisive mother reluctantly embraced her daughter's journey.

The young prodigy was now on a trajectory that would take her beyond the streets of Spanish Town. In 2015, Bunny earned a spot on the senior Jamaican national team, and her prowess on the field and unyielding determination off it caught the attention of football scouts in the USA. She was offered a football scholarship at the University of Tennessee.

She took it straight away, and despite the distance from her Caribbean roots, she embraced the challenge academically and athletically. Shaw graduated with a degree in communications, becoming the first in her family to achieve a university education. Her parents were beaming with pride.

One of the highlights of Bunny's journey came in 2019 when The Reggae Girlz (Chapter 3), as the Jamaican national women's team is affectionately known, secured qualification for the 2019 World Cup. They defeated Panama in a gripping penalty shootout and achieved what no other women's Caribbean football national team had done before.

The 2019 World Cup was a dream come true for Bunny Shaw. Surrounded by jubilant teammates, she savoured the sweet taste of competing at football's marquee event. The journey from Spanish Town to the world stage was complete, and Jamaica celebrated a historic moment in women's football. Unfortunately, they were knocked out in the group stages of the 2019 World Cup in France.

Having had a life marked by unwavering determination, Bunny Shaw and her teammates were back at it again in 2023. They qualified for the Australia and New

Zealand 2023 World Cup despite fighting a battle on their own turf — the Jamaica Football Federation showing reluctance to support the women's team as much as they did the men's.

The inequality encouraged the Jamaican women's team to do something not even the men's national team had done before. It also saw Bunny hit new highs with The Reggae Girlz. This defining moment in Jamaican football history marked the highlight of Shaw's career.

It happened when they secured a historic draw over Brazil in the group stages of the 2023 World Cup — propelling them into the second round! They became the first Caribbean nation, regardless of gender, to achieve this feat. In the process, they ousted Marta ([Chapter 32](#)), widely regarded as the greatest female player of *all time*, from the tournament. The Reggae Girlz firmly established Jamaica's presence on the global football stage during that memorable winter 2023 World Cup. Bunny Shaw's story inspired countless young girls in Jamaica and worldwide. Bunny proved that dreams could be realised through determination and hard work, no matter how improbable. Her words echo with perseverance and encouragement for young girls. "Failure is not permanent. Keep pushing. Keep working hard," she reflects.

Bunny knows the importance of giving back, so she collects discarded boots from her Manchester City teammates. When she returns to Jamaica, she donates them to impoverished children in her home country. Having had to play football in her school shoes because she couldn't afford boots, she understands the struggles of young Jamaican girls who aspire to play football but lack the resources.

The journey from playing football in school shoes to becoming Jamaica's all-time top goal scorer was challenging, but Bunny Shaw eventually emerged victorious. Her story is not just about goals scored, or games won; it's about empowering the next generation of female athletes. In every sprint, in every goal, Bunny Shaw exemplifies the indomitable spirit of a woman who turned impossible dreams into extraordinary realities.

CHAPTER 16
HOPE POWELL — POWERING THROUGH THE GLASS CEILING

FEW WOMEN IN GLOBAL SPORT HAVE SHOWN THE RUGGED determination and resilience that Hope Powell showed en route to becoming one of England's most influential women in football.

Born on December 8, 1966, in Lewisham, London, Hope Patricia Powell's football journey began at a young age and with plenty of obstacles. Much like Bunny Shaw ([Chapter 15](#)), Hope's Jamaican mother strongly disapproved of a young girl playing football—it was simply *not* what was done in Jamaican culture, and it presented severe challenges for a girl who was quickly falling in love with The Beautiful Game.

Undeterred by her mother and inspired by football legends like Kevin Keegan and Ray Wilkins, she dedicated herself to the sport, spending countless hours kicking the ball until dusk fell.

The hours of practice on the concrete pitches of South East London paid off when she got a call to play for her school's boy's team. Powell helped her team win, but she was told that she wouldn't be able to play again for them. The losing team had complained to The Football Association about there being a girl on the team!

Powell was only 11 years old at this point. Much like the Dick, Kerr Ladies before her, she was dealt a hammer blow by The English Football Association, which rules inexplicably barred her from playing on her school team with boys.

That didn't stop Powell, and her breakthrough came when she followed a friend to a training session with the Millwall Lionesses, a women's football team she had only just found out about. It was a pivotal moment that changed the course of her life. Surrounded by other girls who shared her passion for football, Hope felt a sense of belonging and purpose like never before. Despite the initial disapproval from her family, she continued to pursue her dreams with incredible determination.

Hope Powell's talent and dedication soon caught the attention of scouts. At just 16, she received her first call-up to the England Women's national team. It was a dream come true for the young football player who had always believed in her abilities.

Being pitted against the best women in the world showed Powell that while she had the technical ability to compete, she needed to push herself harder to become the best. At a time when elite women football players only trained twice a week, Powell asked the Millwall coaches to design a program just for her. It was a fitness program that saw her train almost every day of the week.

To push herself as hard as she could, she pounded the concrete pavements of South East London with daily runs to get fitter and more robust — human knees, it turns out, weren't designed for that kind of treatment. In her old age, it eventually cost Powell the proper use of her knees.

However, Hope's career soared to new heights from that moment on, and she represented her country internationally.

She would go on to achieve 60 caps in a distinguished career with England — the marquee appearance coming in the 1984 final of what is now the European Women's Championship. England was defeated at the hands of Sweden, which was no surprise as both nations had *very* different approaches to women's football at the time: Sweden had an established women's football team. The England women's team had a sort of routine: they came together on a Friday when they had an international fixture. They would train for a bit on Saturday. They would then play on a Sunday before disbanding immediately after.

Perhaps this lack of investment from the English FA would see her solidify her legacy in women's football.

In 1998, Hope Powell made history as the first female coach of the England Women's national team. At 31, she was tasked with leading and transforming the team, a challenge she embraced wholeheartedly. Despite facing skepticism and doubt from others, Hope remained steadfast in her belief as manager and the team's potential. She also had a vision for the future of women's football.

Under her leadership, the England Women's team achieved unprecedented success, reaching the finals of major tournaments and earning the respect of the football world. While Powell didn't quite reach the heights of a major tournament victory, she laid the foundation that allowed future Lionesses like the ones of 2022 (Chapter 11) to emerge as European champions.

Hope's impact can be seen in how she broke down barriers to pave the way for future generations of female coaches and players. When she took over the England job, Powell didn't have dreads, but she grew them while at The FA to make a statement, to show that she was representing black people from everywhere in England—a true testament to her ambition to help women in football break down barriers.

This resilience saw Powell inspire countless individuals throughout her illustrious career, like Fara Williams (Chapter 12), who would achieve incredible things! Her journey from a young girl playing football on the streets of South London to becoming a pioneering coach and manager is an excellent example of the power of perseverance and self-belief.

While in charge of England, Powell showed that tiny actions can have enormous repercussions for future generations. Something as little as asking her bosses for more footballs at training then snowballed into huge initiatives, like creating national youth teams to expand the reach of football amongst girls. Powell did all this while in charge of the English Women's team. She also demanded more international matches so that England could bridge the gap with elite women's teams like the USA, Germany, and Sweden. If they were to meet the Swedes again, at least now they'd be competing on an even platform that would become the benchmark for thousands of future Lionesses.

Hope Powell was awarded an OBE in 2002 and a CBE in 2010 in recognition of her contribution to the sport. Her story reminds us that anything is possible with hard work, dedication, and a never-say-never attitude. Whether on the football pitch or in life, Hope's message to young girls is clear: dream big, chase your passions, and never be afraid to break barriers and defy expectations.

CHAPTER 17
LILY PARR — THE JEWEL IN DKL'S CROWN

ONCE UPON A TIME, IN THE EARLY 20TH CENTURY, FOOTBALL was deemed a game reserved *only* for men. The Football Association, the governing body of English football, enforced a ban on women playing the sport, believing it was "quite unsuitable" for them. But amidst these challenges, a remarkable player named Lily Parr emerged, whose story would inspire generations of young women and change the future of women's football forever.

Lily Parr was born in St Helens, England, on April 26, 1905. Growing up when society believed football was not for girls, Lily defied expectations and pursued her passion for The Beautiful Game. She played football in the streets with her brothers, perfecting her skills and dreaming of becoming a professional player one day.

As World War I swept the world, men were called to serve their countries, leaving empty factories and workplaces behind. Women like Lily stepped up to fill these roles, taking on jobs traditionally held by men. It was during this time that Lily joined Dick, Kerr & Co.. This locomotive factory had transitioned to producing munitions for the war effort.

Despite the societal norms at the time that discouraged women from playing sports, Lily continued to play football, joining the company's team as a left-back at just 15 years old. Her natural talent and determination quickly caught the attention of her teammates and opponents alike. With her powerful left foot and towering stature of 5 feet 10 inches, Lily became a force to be reckoned with on the field.

In 1921, Lily's star began to shine even brighter. She scored a hat trick (three goals in a single match) in a game against Nelson — it turned out the quick full-back had an eye for goal! At this point, it became apparent she was more suited to being a striker than a left-back. She moved up the field, and her performances started to draw crowds of thousands, with spectators marvelling at her skill and athleticism.

However, Lily's journey was not without its challenges. The Football Association's ban on women's football in 1921 threatened to derail her career before it had even begun. The ban prohibited women from playing in stadiums owned by association clubs, effectively crippling their opportunities to compete at a professional level.

Lily refused to be deterred. Alongside her teammates at Dick, Kerr Ladies Football Club (<u>Chapter 1</u>), Lily continued to play wherever she could find a space to showcase her talent. Despite the ban, the team embarked on tours abroad and played in front of smaller crowds, determined to keep the spirit of women's football alive.

Throughout her illustrious career, Lily amassed an incredible record of achievements. She scored an estimated 1,000 goals during her time with Dick, Kerr Ladies Football Club. Let that sink in. One *thousand* goals! In doing so, Parr became one of the most prolific goal scorers of her era — or anyone else's, for that matter. Her contributions to the team's success were immeasurable, and she was celebrated alongside her teammates as they dominated the women's — and sometimes the men's — football scene.

In 1965, Lily retired from her full-time job in nursing, marking the end of an era in women's football. A few years later, she was diagnosed with breast cancer and underwent a double mastectomy. Despite her health struggles, Lily lived to see the ban on women's football lifted in 1971, which allowed future generations of girls to play the game she so dearly loved.

Today, Lily Parr's legacy lives on as a testament to the resilience and determination of women in sports. Historical markers and museum displays commemorate her achievements, ensuring her story will never be forgotten. Even in 2019, Parr set national records in England, becoming the first woman commemorated with a statue at the National Football Museum in Manchester. She remains an inspiration to young women around the world, reminding them that with hard work and dedication, they can achieve the goals they set out to conquer.

As we reflect on Lily Parr's incredible journey, we are reminded that the path to success is often paved with obstacles. But like Lily, we can overcome challenges and defy expectations to achieve our dreams. Her story teaches us that true greatness knows no boundaries and that perseverance can change the world.

So, to all the young women reading this, remember Lily Parr's story. Let her courage and tenacity inspire you to chase your dreams, both on and off the field. For in the game of life, as in football, the most splendid victories often come from the unlikeliest heroes.

CHAPTER 18
MIA HAMM — THE GOAL-GETTING GREAT

With Lily Parr (Chapter 17) laying down the foundations for women to become global football stars, one woman went further. She cemented the women's game into the highest echelons of world football. Her name echoes with the thunderous applause of victory and the reverent whispers of admiration.

Mia Hamm was a titan of The Beautiful Game. Her journey from a young girl with a dream to an international football icon is a testament to her resilience, determination, and unyielding pursuit of excellence.

From the moment she first laced up her boots to the final whistle of her illustrious career, Mia blazed a trail that inspired millions of young girls to chase their dreams on and off the football field. At a time when women's football was teetering with relative obscurity, her skill and penchant for goals made sure women's football would forever be talked about in the same breath as that of their male counterparts.

Born on March 17, 1972, in Selma, Alabama, Mia Hamm's early years were marked by a love for football that burned brighter than the Alabama sun.

Hamm couldn't have shown her determination to overcome obstacles earlier, as she was born with a club foot, which had to be corrected early on. A club foot is when one's foot grows sideways — almost at a 90-degree angle to the other foot.

Despite this challenge and societal norms that frowned upon girls playing sports, Mia refused to be sidelined. She took to the football field with a ferocity and passion that belied her young age, leaving opponents in awe and spectators breathless.

At just 15 years old, Mia made history as the youngest player to don the U.S. Women's National Soccer Team jersey. It was a moment that would set the stage for a career filled with unprecedented success and unrivalled achievement. From winning two Olympic gold medals for her country to capturing four NCAA titles with the University of North Carolina, Mia's list of accolades reads like a who's who of football greatness.

There aren't many players in the history of the sport (male or female) who have had a more successful decade than Mia had in the 1990s. She won the World Cup held in China in 1991, and to top off her remarkable decade, she won it again on home turf when the USA hosted the World Cup in 1999. These victories, together with the

Olympic gold medal of 1996, catapulted her into global fame.

But Mia's impact extended far beyond the confines of the football pitch. She was more than just a player – she quickly became a role model for young girls everywhere. Her journey inspired a generation of female athletes to reach for the top. Before global names like Serena Williams became household names, Mia paved the way for future athletes from any sport to achieve all their goals. She was a woman with a mission to reach the top and showed unbridled determination to get there.

Her endorsements with Nike and Pepsi helped put the women's game on a level pegging with other established sports. She was doing for football what Michael Jordan and Tiger Woods were doing for basketball and golf. At a time when young girls couldn't resonate with the male-dominated landscape of sport, Mia Hamm was changing that. One goal at a time, trophy after trophy. Simply put, Mia enabled many young women to realise, "I can do sports, too."

Hamm's legacy is not just about the goals she scored or the trophies she won; it's about the countless lives she touched and the dreams she ignited within young girls' hearts worldwide.

What is extraordinary about Mia's impact on women's football is that it transcended geographical barriers. For the first time, female football players were not just being celebrated in their own countries — she was an authentic influencer on a *global* scale. Hamm was at the helm of igniting the popularity of women's football across all seven continents. Much like future iconic athletes Lionel Messi and Cristiano Ronaldo, Mia carved out her own space in the world of football, inspiring a legion of fans and aspiring players with her skill, determination, and unrelenting commitment to excellence.

Like most of the women featured in this book, Mia also used her football talent to foster greatness outside the football pitch. She continued to champion opportunities for women in sports long after she hung up her boots. From founding and heading women's football leagues to advocating for gender equality and equal pay in sports, Mia's commitment to empowering women and girls in sports is a legacy that inspires future generations, even long after her retirement.

As Nike founder Phil Knight noted, Mia Hamm added a new dimension to women's football, elevating the sport to new heights and inspiring millions of girls to dream big and chase their passions.

Hamm's legacy is not just a chapter in the history of women's football. She single-handedly created a tsunami of empowerment for millions of young girls in the USA — girls who — thanks to Mia — dared to dream of a future filled with endless possibilities. Girls like Alex Morgan (Chapter 19), a young girl from California who grew up watching Mia Hamm play ball.

CHAPTER 19
ALEX MORGAN — STRIKING FOR CHANGE

As the illustrious Mia Hamm reigned supreme in women's football, a young Californian girl, Alex Morgan, watched in admiration, ignited by the ambition to mirror her idol's triumphs with the U.S. women's national team. Fortunately, Morgan's resolve was matched by her extraordinary talent with a football and an uncanny ability to find the back of the net — a rare sight on the football field.

Raised in a nurturing environment, Alex's love for football blossomed under her father's tutelage. He was her first coach. With a steady commitment to training from an early age, she secured her spot on her school's football team. She caught the attention of scouts, earning a place in the US Under-20 Women's National Team at a mere 17 years old.

Despite encountering stereotypes in a male-dominated sport, Alex refused to be constrained by societal norms. She challenged the notion that women should adhere to a specific playing style and instead embraced her unique abilities. With grit and determination, she shattered the 'playing like a girl' stereotype, proving that gender is no barrier to success on the field.

One pivotal moment in Morgan's journey occurred during a match against the men's national team, during which she suffered a ligament injury. Alex refused to yield to adversity — she battled through the pain and setback, emerging from the injury stronger and more committed than ever. Alex's resilience is a poignant reminder that obstacles are meant to be overcome, not succumbed to.

At 23, Alex Morgan mirrored Mia Hamm's record of becoming the only woman to score over 20 goals and assist more than 20 others in a single calendar year. She was emulating her childhood hero, showing girls all across America that she was the essence of determination and resilience. Morgan took on Hamm's legacy as a global icon in doing so. As a matter of fact, she went further than her idol.

Morgan achieved unparalleled success, clinching two World Cups with the USA and an Olympic gold medal in 2012. She also amassed numerous accolades at the club level, including becoming an NWSL League champion and a UEFA Champions League winner with Lyon.

Beyond her on-field accolades, Alex's advocacy for gender equality in sports sets her apart. Following the 2015 USA women's football team's World Cup victory, she spearheaded the #EqualPlayEqualPay movement, demanding equal treatment and respect for female athletes worldwide. Her endeavours culminated in a historic $24 million settlement in May 2022, ensuring equal pay for male and female U.S. players.

This set a precedent for women athletes across various sports and kickstarted a movement that echoed across many different countries worldwide. Morgan, along with Rapinoe (Chapter 13) and a few other U.S. teammates, had transcended the sport and impacted countless athletes worldwide.

Her determination to inspire young girls was evident when she authored "The Kicks," a book series tailored to middle schoolers. The series offers relatable tales about football and its lessons on teamwork and perseverance. As a co-founder of a digital media company, she amplifies women's voices and advocates for meaningful change. She champions clean nutrition and healthy living through partnerships with brands like Orgain, inspiring others to focus on their well-being.

Despite her hectic schedule, Alex Morgan prioritises her role as a mother to her 2-year-old daughter, Charlie. Leading by example, her life has already demonstrated the significance of ambition, drive, and resilience to Charlie in the hope that she, too, will challenge societal norms one day.

Alex Morgan's journey epitomises the potency of determination, fighting for what is right, and advocacy for future generations. Aspiring young athletes can draw inspiration from her remarkable life, striving to impact their communities positively and beyond. Alex's legacy as a champion of equality and inspiration continues to ignite the aspirations of future women sports stars, urging them to pursue their dreams and challenge the status quo.

CHAPTER 20
MICHELLE AKERS — TRUE GIANT OF THE GAME

It would be remiss of us to discuss Megan Rapinoe (Chapter 13), Mia Hamm (Chapter 18), and Alex Morgan (Chapter 19) without acknowledging the giant whose shoulders these ladies stood upon to achieve greatness.

This giant, figuratively and literally standing at an imposing 5'10", was one of the earliest pioneers of the U.S. women's game: Michelle Akers.

Born on the 1st of February 1966 in Santa Clara, California, Michelle grew up playing football with her brothers. The tough love shown by her brothers moulded her from an early age into a no-nonsense defender. With no girls' teams in her hometown, she had to play with the boys and match their aggression if she wanted to compete. And compete she did - fighting tooth and nail for every aerial ball and challenge in the box.

When the family moved to Washington State, Akers went down to the Seattle Sounders ground every weekend to watch her local team battle it out in the men's professional football league. There, she was mesmerised by an unlikely hero named David Gillet, an old-school Scottish defender. He played no-thrills football, was efficient and not flashy, and was aggressive but fair. Most importantly, he wasn't the most gifted player, so his work ethic had to be higher than anyone else's on the pitch to compete.

Akers fell in love with his combination of a high work ethic coupled with an aggressive approach on the field, and it would go on to define her success on the pitch. It was on the fields of Shorecrest High School, replicating Gillet's style, where she honed her skills and showcased her natural talent, earning her the recognition of an 'All-American' three times during high school. All-American is an honour bestowed upon only the best American amateur athletes.

Michelle's journey continued at the University of Central Florida, where she excelled through sheer hard work. After the women's team's training finished, she would always stay behind to train with the men's team, improving every aspect of her game to match that of her male counterparts. It wasn't long before she was *better* than her university male counterparts.

Her hard work paid off to the extent that she was given a new position on the field—she went from a hard-tackling defender to a rock-solid striker in charge of scoring goals. And scoring goals she did, netting the U.S. Women's National Team's first-ever goal. It would be the first of many for Akers.

From her debut in 1985 to her retirement in 2000,

she became a driving force behind the U.S. Women's National Team's success, leading them to victory in the first-ever Women's World Cup in 1991. Michelle's performance in China that winter, including being the tournament's top scorer with ten goals and firing the U.S. to victory over Norway in the final, solidified her status as more than a football legend. Her manager called her an "iconic warrior without weaknesses" at the time, and few could argue against that.

That winter in 1991, Akers firmly put the USA on the football map, achieving a feat that the men's national team had never done before (and, at the time of writing, seem unlikely to achieve). Yet, something didn't sit right with Akers. They were made to train on concrete pitches before their World Cup victory and were forced to wear hand-me-down jerseys from the men's national team.

Something needed to be done for justice and equality to prevail. In 1996, Akers and her team went on strike to demand equal bonus pay as their male counterparts. The dispute was quickly settled, and Akers brought home the Gold Medal for Team USA. Unbeknownst to her then, she ignited the spark that would eventually fuel the ongoing fight for equality championed by Rapinoe and Morgan twenty years later.

Despite facing numerous injuries throughout her career, including a torn medial collateral ligament and a dislocated shoulder, Michelle never wavered in her determination to succeed. Befitting of the extraordinary woman that Akers was, one of her latest acts in a USA jersey was captaining her country to a second World Cup victory in 1999. She embodies for all aspiring athletes that setbacks are simply opportunities for growth and perseverance.

In 2002, Michelle was honoured as the FIFA Female Player of the Century, a title she shared with China's Sun Wen. This prestigious award recognised her exceptional talent and her lasting impact on the sport of football. Michelle's induction into the National Soccer Hall of Fame in 2004 further solidified her legacy as one of the greatest players in the game's history. She was one of only two women in Pelé's list of the 125 greatest living football players.

As teenage girls aspiring to greatness, we can look to Michelle Akers as an example of what it means to shine through adversity. Having mastered two positions and overcome not only nasty injuries but also the inequalities women faced late in the 20th century, her journey is a reminder that reaching one's goals can be easily achieved with grit, determination, and resilience.

She is more than a football legend; she is the giant who inspired the most incredible female football players of the 21st century.

CHAPTER 21
SUSAN WHELAN — THE GENIUS BEHIND ENGLISH FOOTBALL'S GREATEST TRIUMPH

In the realm of football, 2016 will always be remembered as the year of the most improbable triumph in the men's game.

That year, a modest club from Leicester, England, shattered insurmountable odds by clinching the English Premier League title, triumphing over global giants such as Manchester City, Manchester United, and Liverpool along the way.

And while manager Claudio Ranieri and his boys took all the plaudits for what they had done on the pitch, a delighted woman sat in the Director's Box of the King Power Stadium. She didn't require, nor did she want, any recognition or praise. She was happy that all her hard work and dedication in assembling that team had just paid off.

Chief Executive Officers don't come any better than Susan Whelan.

In a male-dominated world where shouting the

loudest seems a prerequisite to being recognised, Whelan quietly goes about her day-to-day — letting her actions do the talking. Winning the Premier League after just five years of assuming her role, despite facing 5000-1 odds, is the most powerful statement anyone can make.

The shrewd businesswoman's career began at an early age in Dublin, where she helped her parents run their jewellery shop. This taught her the fundamentals of running a business. She scrutinised profit and loss statements over her morning cornflakes and pored over balance sheets before going to bed.

Outgrowing the family business quickly, her parents encouraged her to expand her horizons, eventually leading her to manage a series of duty-free shops in Thailand. This is where her influence on global football began.

While working at the travel retail group King Power, Susan Whelan ascended through the ranks. When the company acquired Leicester City Football Club, she was appointed the club's leader and its Chief Executive Officer.

Coming from a rugby-loving family, Whelan was very open about not knowing much about football. However, her characteristic courage and strength in conducting business emerged as she bravely accepted the role and began familiarising herself with the sport's intricacies.

Within a couple of years, she had taken the club from mid-table mediocrity in the second tier of English football to competing with the biggest clubs in world football in the Premier League.

Whelan achieved this by assembling what many consider the most fantastic group of scouts in the history of the English Premier League. Their mission was to unearth football talents who were diamonds in the rough, potential future world champions whose abilities had yet to be fully recognised. Additionally, they targeted players who were perceived to be past their prime but had yet to be given a fair opportunity. Through this approach, Whelan instilled a culture of vision and optimism at Leicester FC, transforming the club's outlook in ways previously unseen.

Her scouts eventually assembled players like Mahrez, Vardy, Chillwell, and Drinkwater under one club. Perhaps most important was the arrival of future World Cup winner N'golo Kante — the defensive lynchpin of the Leicester City midfield who enabled the rest of the team to valiantly and freely trudge forward to score match-winning goals. Much like Whelan, Kante did his job quietly, diligently, and extraordinarily.

Having this array of talent never promises success in the Premier League. After all, the EPL is the league where the most colossal names in global football compete. So it was no surprise that Leicester City, despite recruiting good players, almost got relegated to the second tier of English football in 2015. Because of this near relegation, bookmakers gave them near-impossible odds of winning the Premier League in 2016.

True to her character, Whelan dug deep within

herself to give Leicester City the best chance possible to compete in the Premier League. Implementing shrewd marketing and merchandising strategies, she generated sufficient revenue to attract a high-profile manager, Claudio Ranieri.

This decision demonstrated her tenacity in the face of adversity. It went against most fans' wishes, as their previous manager, Nigel Pearson, had successfully led them into the Premiership only a few months earlier. It was a bold move by Whelan that could have easily backfired. Yet, few women are as savvy, brave, and shrewd in business as she is.

It turned out Ranieri was the final piece of the puzzle in Whelan's assembly of the most extraordinary team English football has ever seen.

From Operations to Accounts, Marketing, Branding, and even the canteen staff, Whelan assembled a workforce at Leicester City Football Club to propel the men's first team to achieve the single most extraordinary feat English football had ever seen.

Having arguably played the most prominent role in assembling Leicester City's 2016 winning team, a humble Whelan remained actively out of the limelight. It wasn't until she received an honorary doctorate in law that she gave a slight glimpse into her unassuming drive and determination: "Be the person who does the right thing. Even when no one is looking."

And, using an analogy of learning to swim, her message to young girls with big dreams is simple: "Go a little bit out of your depth, and when you don't feel that your feet are quite touching the bottom, you are just about in the right place to do something exciting."

In the case of Susan Whelan, it doesn't get more exciting than manufacturing the greatest accomplishment that any English football team has ever seen.

CHAPTER 22
CHAN YUEN TING — SHOWING THEM HOW IT'S DONE

While Whelan's effort in assembling the biggest underdogs in the history of the sport must be given all the merit it deserves, not even the most ardent of football fans will remember that Leicester City's 5000-1 triumph in the Premier League was perhaps not *the* football story of 2016.

An event in Hong Kong, merely a month before Leicester were crowned champions of England, would have ripple effects that were more far-reaching for women's football than Whelan's heroic Leicester efforts. This was because it was the *first time* an event like this happened.

Women's football has undeniably advanced since its inception in the 19th century and the Dick Kerr Ladies era of the early 20th century. While numerous barriers and prejudices were dismantled in the early 21st century, one significant milestone remained unattained: a woman managing a team of men to become top-flight champions of their country. That changed when Chan Yuen Ting took charge of Eastern FC in the Hong Kongese professional football league.

As with many of the heroines in this book, Chan's parents wanted her to pursue a career different from football. They encouraged her to become a teacher instead. Not only were her parents against sports as a career, but they also disapproved of her playing the game. However, Chan's passion for the sport burned so brightly that her first hurdle was overcoming her family's disappointment regarding her chosen vocation. This was a challenging task for her, yet it was necessary to forge her name in the history books of the football world.

Chan's journey in the game grew from a genuine admiration for the way David Beckham played the game of football. From there, she achieved a Masters in Sports Science and Health Management before landing her first job as a video analyst for Hong Kongese professional football club Pegasus FC.

Chan honed her tactical skills in football while working as a video analyst. After countless hours watching and replaying various movements from Pegasus and their opponents, she realised that football games could be won with solid tactics diligently executed by the players on the pitch.

Chan juggled her role as a video analyst with pursuing coaching licenses from the Asian Football Federation. Again, driven by her love for the game, this decision would change the course of women's football history.

Having the coaching license meant that Eastern FC knocked at her door when they needed a new manager. Chan was scared. She had been working in the Hong Kongese Premier League for five years. Still, she had been behind the scenes in Pegasus's tactical department. Being approached to be the Manager and Head Coach of one of the leading teams in Hong Kong was a different kettle of fish. She would be thrown into the spotlight in a male-dominated world without any experience at the job she was hired to do.

But, taking a leaf out of Susan Whelan's book (Chapter 21) – something that every woman featured in this book has undoubtedly done – she got comfortable with feeling out of her depth. She took on the role with bravery and diligence.

Chan has often spoken about feeling nervous and scared when taking on the top role at one of the leading teams in Hong Kong. This fear stemmed not only from her lack of experience as a manager but also from the fact that, at only 27, she was managing men who were much older and more experienced than her. However, her expertise shone through, and her nerves calmed down after her first game in charge, a convincing 6-1 victory over local rivals South China!

Modesty personifies Chan, and as she continued to rack up victories in charge of Eastern FC, she often attributed most of her success to the manager who had preceded her and moved on to another club. However, the reality is that effective management goes beyond tactics; it's about instilling a clear vision in all your players and extracting the best from them so that they all work together towards a common goal.

And that is precisely what Chan did. A mere five months after being at the helm of Eastern FC, her team went to South China FC and beat them 2-1. That victory sealed Eastern FC's 2016 Hong Kong Premier League title. It was the first time they had won the league in 21 years, and in doing so, Chan Yuen Ting wrote herself into the Guinness Book of World Records by becoming the first woman to win a top-flight title in men's professional football.

Chan's journey is unique in world football, and much like the Dick Kerr Ladies before her, she stands alone as a global pioneer. A shining example to girls everywhere that no matter how nervous, scared, or unprepared they may feel, through hard work and self-belief, they can achieve anything they set their minds to. Even in a male-dominated world like football, belief and hard work will break even the most seemingly impossible barriers.

Chan Yuen Ting stands out as a pioneer in women's football. Despite her relatively recent achievements, they will undoubtedly be recognised as the catalyst for an era where male and female managers globally compete at the same level. While this equality may not have been fully realised yet, Chan Yuen Ting's forward-thinking approach highlights just how ahead of her time she truly is.

CHAPTER 23
JACQUI OATLEY — MOULDING THE PERCEPTION OF MILLIONS

IF CHAN YUEN TING'S HEROICS IN CHINA (CHAPTER 22) pioneered a new way of thinking, then Jacqui Oatley's influence in England, the other founding country of football, cannot go unmentioned.

And funnily enough, much like Chan, it was at the age of 27 that Jacqui Oatley's influence on football began to materialise. You see, at this age, Oatley decided a much-needed professional change was in order. This decision came after a devastating knee injury forced Oatley to reassess the direction of her football career.

Jacqui Oatley was an amateur football player who loved the sport. She would work as a Sales and Marketing Manager by day. At night, she would quench her insatiable thirst for football by playing for Chiswick Ladies Football Club in London.

After suffering a debilitating knee injury while playing for her team, she was told she'd be out of the game for ten months. Ten months without football is ten months too long for a lover of the game, so she took the drastic action of flipping her whole life around so it revolved around the sport.

She decided to change her career and train as a journalist.

If her injury prevented her from playing the sport, this new decision would allow her to cover the sport from the stands. It was a decision that would touch the lives of hundreds of millions of people worldwide.

After earning her journalism degree, she gradually progressed up the ranks of the BBC. The BBC, short for the British Broadcasting Corporation, is one of the first broadcasting companies in the world and arguably the most prestigious and trusted broadcaster globally. Within the U.K., the BBC hosts a flagship football program called Match Of The Day, which is how most British people consume the country's national sport, football.

On April 21, 2007, Jacqui Oatley made history by becoming the first woman in the U.K. to commentate on a men's professional football match. A seemingly innocuous event that would have enormous consequences for women like Fara Williams (Chapter 12) and other professional athletes.

Sadly, never before 2007 had a woman been seen or heard publicly commenting on a professional male football game in England. It shouldn't have been such a big deal in 21st-century England, but the decision to have a woman commentate on a male sport initially sent shockwaves around the male-dominated sport. People, purely based on Oatley's gender, questioned her credentials and ability to do her job.

As with all the women mentioned in this book, Oatley persevered through unjust criticism, showing her tenacity and grit in facing adversity. Oatley felt isolated and mistreated by the criticism. In an era where social media trolls were starting to appear by the thousands, Oatley had to dig deep and believe in her ability. Her mental strength was being tested, and she needed to change her perspective to come through the other side unscathed. That's why she focused on the privilege of being able to commentate for the BBC instead of faceless online bullies who were trying to derail her career.

Oatley's perseverance was only outmatched by her talent as a football commentator. Clearly an avid connoisseur of the game, she became an established commentator of football matches in England. In doing so, she inspired thousands of girls to pursue their journalistic dreams in a male-dominated culture. A growing generation of female football lovers looked up to Oatley as a beacon of inspiration in pursuing a career in the sport outside of the playing field.

More critical than inspiring these young girls, however, is the seed that Oatley planted in the social fabric of how most people viewed the sport. Until Oatley made female commentary mainstream, there was an element of football being treated as a "Boys Club" around the world.

Oatley helped change gender inequalities in all sports — going on to commentate on other sports like snooker, golf, and MotoGP. But it's the indelible mark that she left in football commentating that paved the way for commentators like Fara Williams to be seen and heard as equals when commentating on global events like the men's FIFA World Cup. Oatley opened the door of opportunity to hundreds of female broadcasters worldwide - reaching an even bigger audience when she became the first woman to commentate on a U.S. broadcast of the Men's FIFA World Cup in 2022.

She was appointed a Member of the Order of the British Empire (MBE) in 2016 for services to broadcasting and diversity in sport in the U.K. However, the biggest accolade that can be given to her is the recognition she deserves for showing the courage to pursue a path that had never before been trodden by a woman. She was brave enough to step into a press box at a time when men sadly assumed that if a woman was in a press box, she was either bringing the tea or, at best, was the wife of one of the male commentators in the press box.

She fought through societal hardships that would weigh most people down and, through her tenacity and drive, used her platform to defy a hundred-year-plus-old notion that football was a male-only sport. Jacqui Oatley changed that, one word at a time, game after game, tournament after tournament, making football a much more inclusive sport. A sport that millions of women worldwide can now more easily relate to every time they hear Oatley's commentary on TV.

CHAPTER 24
GURINDER CHADHA — MASTER OF THE MAINSTREAM

JACQUI OATLEY (CHAPTER 23) ISN'T ALONE IN BREAKING mainstream barriers in the history of women's sport in Britain — Gurinder Chadha can proudly stand alongside her. And while Chadha is a filmmaker and not *directly* involved in football, her role and reach in British football must be recognised!

Chadha is the director of the 2002 film Bend It Like Beckham. Although released over twenty years ago, this film continues to profoundly impact young girls, especially girls of ethnic minorities in European countries, who want to pursue their dreams of being involved in football.

Although 2002 doesn't seem like that long ago, the football landscape for women was a very different and hostile place back then. First, women's football wasn't even a professional sport in the UK when Chadha released her film. So, much like all the extraordinary women in this book, Chadha was ahead of her time when she blazed the trail which inspired millions of young girls to take up the sport.

"Bend It Like Beckham" tells the story of Jess, a British-Indian girl who grapples with embracing her Indian heritage while staying true to her love of the game. In that inner fight, Chadha beautifully encapsulates the common thread that most women in this book have had: a struggle with their parents to let them pursue their dreams in a sport they love.

The low-budget film was an instant success. It spoke to millions of girls around the country who felt alone simply because they loved a sport discouraged by parents and dominated by men. Chadha's film inspired a generation of women, predominantly black and Asian girls, to break free from the shackles of trepidation and pursue the game they loved.

The film was released 30 years after the English FA lifted its ban on women playing football, and sadly, not much progress had been made in the women's game in that time. Twenty years after the film's release, Chadha achieved something that had only been seen before in England with the likes of Beatlemania. The uptake in girls' participation shot up so dramatically that by 2020, there were 3.4 million girls playing football in the UK. While this was helped by The FA's "Gameplan for Growth," it would be remiss not to mention the invaluable effort that Chadha's masterpiece had in changing how girls viewed the game.

Chadha's film was a bastion of hope and inspiration for millions of girls who realised that football was also their game - that their love for a game that at the time was male-dominated wasn't something to be ashamed of, but celebrated.

Put simply, her film epitomised the power of representation and changed the collective sentiment of a new generation. A generation that would inherently become more accepting of women in the sport. A generation that would likely be outraged by the collective societal attitudes of the forefathers before them.

Chadha's courage to not only dream but to showcase a world where women's football captured the hearts and minds of everyone in the country paved the way for the English Lionesses of 2022 (Chapter 11). This extraordinary group of women would have been young girls when they first got inspired by Chadha's film. They would make Chadha's dream a reality for every man and woman living in England in the summer of 2022 when they brought home the European Championship.

In less than two hours, Chadha achieved what thousands of girls had dreamed of for decades. She dispelled the myth that football was only a man's sport and played a pivotal role in getting the British public to embrace the women's game.

Gurinder Chadha's film is the football equivalent of scoring a hat-trick in a World Cup Final. And for that, she is to be celebrated with the same passion and fanfare, if not more, as all of the other football players in this book.

CHAPTER 25
KARREN BRADY — THE FIRST LADY OF FOOTBALL

VERY MUCH LIKE SUSAN WHELAN (CHAPTER 21), THERE IS ONE incredible woman behind the success of one of English football's most recent European champions.

West Ham United won the Europa Conference League in 2023, with Karren Brady as the club's vice chairman. While she has played a crucial role in stabilising the club, which was previously known for fluctuating between English football's top two tiers, it is her entire career in the football industry that truly sets her apart.

While her upbringing may have provided Brady a leg-up in her entrepreneurial career, the things she has done in business since being provided with the opportunity to shine have been nothing short of remarkable.

When she was 18 years old, she worked for Saatchi & Saatchi, arguably the leading advertising agency in the world, before choosing to work at the London Broadcasting Corporation. There, she met David Sullivan, and her life in football took off.

Sullivan was highly impressed by a young Brady's determination and work ethic. He was so impressed that he jumped at the chance when she jokingly suggested purchasing a struggling football club and entrusting her with its management to turn it around financially!

And so it was, at the young age of 23, amidst a culture dominated by male bravado, that she courageously assumed the position of Managing Director at Birmingham City Football Club. The club, then facing bankruptcy, was rescued and transformed into a financially stable entity under Brady's leadership, eventually yielding substantial profits after just a few years.

Brady had to develop a thick skin early on. Working in a male-dominated industry at a young age, as the leader of men, presented numerous challenges. Despite the chauvinistic environment, she demonstrated resilience and tenacity daily. When faced with inappropriate remarks from a Birmingham City player, Brady's response was swift: she humorously suggested he would be sold to Crewe, a town in northern England with limited football prestige — a club where no elite professional would want to play. Although initially perceived as a joke, the player was indeed transferred to Crewe three days later, showing that Brady was not to be messed about with! She sent a strong message that day.

Under Brady's leadership, Birmingham was promoted to the Premiership. When Sullivan sold the club 17 years later, it was valued at £80m higher than its worth before Brady's transformative reign.

In 2010, she became the vice-chairwoman of West Ham United. She immediately set her sights on solidifying the London club's status as a Premier League team. With relentless determination, she pursued the leasehold of the newly built London Olympic Stadium, aiming to establish the club as a permanent fixture in the league.

Fighting tooth and nail and overcoming stiff competition from Tottenham Hotspur, she secured the leasehold of the stadium for West Ham United. This move increased their match-day capacity from 35,000 to 62,000 spectators, significantly boosting revenue. As a result, the club soared through the Premier League and ultimately in Europe.

In 2023, after Brady had dedicated more than a decade of work for the club, West Ham United achieved victory in the newly formed Europa League. Though it was the third tier of European competition, winning a European trophy was a huge accomplishment! West Ham was crowned Champions of Europe, a feat owed mainly to the tenacity and trailblazing skills of one woman who fought tirelessly in an ego-dominated and often chauvinistic workforce. Karren Brady achieved what many deemed impossible, bringing a European trophy to West Ham United after an agonising 58-year wait. Kudos to Karren and her team.

CHAPTER 26
REBECCA WELCH — WHISTLING HER WAY TO THE TOP

IT'S NOT *JUST* THE FOOTBALL PLAYERS ON THE FIELD WHO CAN inspire women worldwide. As Rebecca Welch stood in the middle of Craven Cottage in London, her heart pounding with excitement and anticipation, she *knew* she was inspiring millions of girls worldwide.

This Premier League game in December 2023 would mark a historic milestone in football, and Welch was right in the thick of it! She was about to become the first woman to referee a Premier League game...

As she blew her whistle to start the beginning of Fulham vs Burnley, she was doing more than just getting a game underway; she was shifting the landscape of sports officiating in the UK, breaking a significant gender barrier in one of the world's most prestigious football leagues.

From her humble beginnings in Washington, England, Welch had embarked on a remarkable journey that had led her to this special occasion. On her path to becoming a referee, the card-wielding, no-nonsense official reminds young girls worldwide that hard work and commitment pay off for anyone who wants to be at the top of their field.

Having started with no real aspirations of reaching the highest level of refereeing, Rebecca Welch's perseverance to be the best at what she does drove her to smash down gender barriers that had unnecessarily lingered in the men's game.

Aside from perhaps Susan Whelan's ([Chapter 21](#)) and Chan Yuen Ting's ([Chapter 22](#)) remarkable achievements in managing male football players to greatness, there are few things scarier than overseeing the conduct of 22 ego-driven males, paid to be competitive, battling it out in the fastest and most-watched league in the world! However, Rebecca Welch took to this challenge like a fish to water, officiating these men seamlessly while being a role model for aspiring female referees worldwide.

Welch's football journey had been fraught with challenges and obstacles from an early age — her biggest challenge being the lack of playing ability for a sport she loved. However, that didn't dissuade her from participating in the game. At 27 years old, she decided to train as a referee, showing courage to pivot and fearlessness in trying something new at an age when most people would consider it too late.

Training to officiate a male sport isn't easy. Your body has to undergo rigorous physical exercise to ensure you're physically fit to keep up with the men who play in one of the fastest leagues in the world. Adding to the challenge, Welch had to balance this demanding training regimen while also working a 9-5 job.

She held an administrative position in the National Healthcare Service in the UK, which required her to juggle both engagements to reach the higher echelons of her refereeing career. This commitment was so significant that it would take Welch nine years to balance both jobs before she could transition to refereeing full-time.

She persevered for almost a decade, driven by her passion for the game and her desire to inspire others. In doing so, she broke many records and achieved many firsts, including becoming the first woman to referee an FA Cup game and the only female English referee at the Women's 2023 World Cup.

Welch's historic career inspires women worldwide, not only those who want to start refereeing but also those fighting for equality in sport. Her path defies stereotypes and illustrates that barriers can be overcome through talent, commitment, and equitable access to opportunities, sowing the seeds for future generations to blossom. As she quite simply puts it: "If you want to do something, just do it. Your biggest power is that **you** are **you**."

CHAPTER 27
STÉPHANIE FRAPPART — FRANCE'S FEARLESS PIONEER

IF WELCH'S CAREER (CHAPTER 26) IS SET TO INSPIRE MILLIONS of future generations of young women, then it is only apt to mention the catalyst for women's refereeing worldwide. The lady who whistled her way to global notoriety and is the female icon of officiating in the men's game: Stéphanie Frappart.

The pinnacle of Frappart's career was when she took charge of the men's European Super Cup final of 2019. On that warm summer's evening in Istanbul in August of 2019, the image of her officiating the best 22 players on Earth was beamed to hundreds of millions across the globe. That moment undoubtedly touched the lives of millions of young girls watching on TV—they could *finally* relate to referees at the highest level.

Stephanie's career was challenging. It took her over twenty years of hard work and dedication to reach the Super Cup Final, smashing glass ceiling after glass ceiling along the way.

Frappart's journey is one of dedication and sacrifice. Growing up in Herblay-sur-Seine, near Paris, her refereeing career faced a significant challenge at 18. Frappart played football on Saturdays and refereed on Sundays, a routine she had maintained since she was only 13. However, at 18, she had to make a crucial decision with significant implications. This decision came as she entered university to study sports.

In her own words, this meant that there was "too much sport" in her life. Something had to give. Fortunately, for millions of young girls whom Frappart would later inspire, what "gave" was her decision to stop playing football. This allowed her to focus on her studies and her journey as a referee.

Her refereeing journey was long, but after almost two decades of hard work climbing the French professional ladders, she made it to the elite levels of men's professional football.

The men's elite professional game is fraught with misogyny, so what Frappart must have endured over 20 years of officiating in the lower leagues, where there's less accountability, should stay out of this book. However, it highlights this impressive woman's resilience and thick skin. This toughness and strength of character make her a beacon of inspiration to countless young girls across the globe – her impact really cannot be overstated.

The European Cup Final in 2019 catapulted her into global stardom and showed everyone around the world just how good she was at her job - it was only a matter of a few months before she was breaking new world records, and in 2021, renowned media outlet L'Equipe named her the most influential figure in French football. At a time when France had Kylian Mbappe, arguably the world's best player at the peak of his powers, Frappart topped the list - showing that football in France was finally a level playing field.

Her reach truly went global in 2022 when she became the first woman to ever referee in a men's World Cup - the greatest sporting event on Earth.

"If you want to referee men's matches, you'd better be at your best on a physical level," Frappart said. Much like Welch, this aspect of her journey deserves recognition. Frappart has dedicated herself to the physical demands required to officiate at the highest level of men's football, pushing herself as hard, if not harder, than the professional male players do.

One could argue that Frappart is not just a referee but also an athlete. At forty years old, she runs 12 kilometres multiple times a week to match the fitness levels of elite football players at the peak of their physical prowess.

Having featured in the 2022 World Cup was Frappart's most significant achievement - it overtook her 2019 Super Cup appearance by a country mile. This is because the 2022 World Cup was a tournament seen by BILLIONS of people. And being seen matters. Boys see it. Men see it. But most importantly, women see it. Women who, for so long, have faced many obstacles on their way to a career in football.

Frappart's remarkable command of players, her physical prowess, and her confident demeanour amidst 22 men on the field are powerful in breaking down the barriers that have hindered girls from pursuing a football career. Her exemplary performances have paved the way for future female referees, ensuring that nothing should stand in their way.

By officiating the most important games in world football, she has smashed preconceived notions about the role of women in not just sport but also society. Thanks to Stéphanie, refereeing will never again be seen as a "man's job"—she has certainly inspired many young ladies to follow her lead.

CHAPTER 28
ENI ALUKO — UNSTOPPABLE SPIRIT

Eniola Aluko was born in Nigeria on February 21, 1987, and relocated to England just six months later. She honed her football skills on the streets of Birmingham, often playing until the late hours of the night with her brother on the concrete pitches of England's second-biggest city.

They would call her "Eddie" when playing so that she would fit in with the boys more. However, it wasn't long before she wasn't fitting in. Eni, it turned out, was *much* better at football than most of the boys and would stand out every time she touched the ball.

From a very early age, Eni started showing the strength and determination that would go on to define her career. Like many of the superb women in this book, she had the most vital role model in her mother, who motivated her to keep living her own path, undeterred by what other people thought. Aluko's mother was pressured by her Nigerian relatives to *discourage* Eni from pursuing her love of football. Driven by a conservative culture, Eni's Nigerian family didn't think football was a sport for girls. They didn't think any sport was fit for girls, but if she had to pick one, tennis would be the right path to go down because it was a sport where you could wear a skirt!

Undeterred by the outdated mentality and shielding her daughter from unnecessary comments, Eni's mum supported a young Aluko to pursue her dreams of becoming a professional football player, and at only 14, she went on to play for the ladies first team of Birmingham City FC. It was the start of an incredible career that would see her play for Chelsea and Juventus.

It would also see the Nigerian-born star get her first England cap. Her role with England would see Aluko fight one of her most significant fights. As a woman of African background, she had to fight misconceptions on *two* fronts as she made her mark on football. One, that the women's game wasn't as good as the men's, but two, and perhaps one that would hurt her more, was that she wasn't really English because she was born in Nigeria. Her strength of character came to the fore yet again. Not only did she thrive with the English team after that first international game, but she went on to represent her country 101 more times, defying the critics with each goal she scored for her country. Back in her country of birth, she was fighting *another* fight, and that was having to justify why she chose to play for England instead of

Nigeria — it would seem that Aluko would not be able to win. But she did. On many different levels.

Eni's career is even more impressive because, much like Nadia Nadim (Chapter 2), she juggled her professional football career with her studies. She graduated from Brunel University with a first-class law degree. A clear understanding of the law and an inherent need to change the face of women's football led her to stand up to the English Football Association.

It is often said that the only thing necessary for evil to triumph is for good people to do nothing. The football world can be a place where these evils translate into casual racism and thinly veiled misogyny, and Aluko decided to *do* something.

She complained to The English Football Association about her manager Mark Sampson's comments about her family coming from Nigeria. They were perhaps innocuous comments in his mind (and the minds of many). Still, Aluko highlighted how inappropriate comments like Sampson's can unfavourably mould how immigrants are seen in the countries they adopt as their home. Sampson left his role as England Women's Manager, and Aluko taught millions a lesson about standing up for what you believe in. Not only did it take courage to stand up to her boss, but it taught a nation that ill-timed jokes or generalisations about someone's race are *never* OK.

Having had a professional football career many would envy, Aluko made her biggest statement as a pundit. In 2014, she became the first woman pundit in the BBC's Match Of The Day. Match Of The Day is the UK's flagship football show, and millions of viewers watch it every Saturday night. For the dreams and aspirations of millions of girls who previously couldn't relate to professional football in the UK, it was important for women to be seen on their television screens.

Aluko's eloquence, intelligence, and passion for the game were evident whenever she appeared in front of the cameras. Her punditry skills were so impressive that the BBC continued to invite her back for more appearances. Much like her numerous goals for England, which contributed to the growing popularity of the women's team, her football knowledge transformed the landscape of British football punditry. Before Aluko, it was rare to see women analysing men's football.

She did this gracefully, much like many other aspects of her life, not without having to fight misconceptions. There were times while discussing the men's 2018 World Cup live on air that other male pundits would applaud her comments. This was undoubtedly due to her impressive football knowledge. However, it also highlighted the inequalities and misconceptions that still existed in the sport. Even if there was no malice in the applause, it underscored women's challenges in commenting on male football. However, Aluko continued to deliver analysis masterclasses to the whole of the UK — slowly but surely becoming a household name.

Aluko, much like Oatley (Chapter 23), made it mainstream and accepted to have both genders openly discuss men's professional football in the UK. Her presence on TV will unquestionably profoundly impact millions of children in playgrounds across the UK. Boys will no longer see girls as anything other than their playing equals, meaning young girls like Eni will no longer have to call themselves "Eddie" to fit in.

CHAPTER 29

REBEKAH STOTT — TESTED BEYOND BELIEF

OF ALL THE STRUGGLES AND TESTS WOMEN IN THIS BOOK HAVE faced, one battle is perhaps the hardest to overcome. It is a fight that 4.4 million women across the world lose every year, and that is the fight against cancer. Rebekah Stott was *determined* not to add to those numbers.

Stott was born in New Zealand and had a ball at her feet from a very early age. It wasn't long before she jumped over the Tasman Sea and debuted in the Australian A League Women's team Brisbane Roar.

Her tough-tackling, no-nonsense defending was so impressive that Melbourne Victory knocked at her door after only one year at Brisbane Roar. Not only did this get her a transfer to one of Australia's leading teams, but the fighting spirit she showed on the football pitch would ultimately save her life and define her incredible career.

After rising through the ranks in Australian football, Stott's career took her to the English Women's Super League, where she represented Brighton & Hove Albion.

The year was 2020, and while most of the world was isolated, Rebekah Stott was ready to come off the traps for her new club and quickly hit the ground running with this new chapter of her career. Unfortunately, life had other plans for her.

She went for constant checkups after finding a lump on her neck. The lump kept getting bigger, and the doctors didn't quite know what was wrong — until a few months later when they gave her the diagnosis of Hodgkin's lymphoma, which is a type of blood cancer.

Cancer is the second biggest killer of humans, with one in six deaths on the planet being caused by the disease. It is a testament to Stott's character that when she was diagnosed with cancer, she was "actually quite relieved."

She took on the disease like she had taken on all the strikers she had encountered in her career: without fear.

Knowing her enemy helped her overcome it, "I was like, 'Yes, we've got this, now I can get onto it and get better,'" she said after hearing of her diagnosis. Talk about being a strong and courageous woman!

Amidst a world retreating into isolation, Stott bravely emerged with news of her battle, reaching out and connecting with an ever-growing audience through a blog documenting her journey. Returning to Australia to confront her cancer head-on, she found herself enveloped in a wave of support from well-wishers near and far.

A couple of months into the disease, which cost her the chance to appear in the Tokyo Olympics, Stotty had lost all her hair. It would seem that the all too sad and common side-effects of cancer were taking a toll on the Kiwi star, but, much like her performances on the pitch, Stott was about to defend with all her might and emerge victorious. She refused to be downtrodden and showed through her blog that it was possible to fight this awful disease with a positive attitude and a smile.

During her battle with cancer, Stott founded a company called Beat It by Stotty, which offers bags filled with comforting items for cancer patients during their hospital stays. Her empathy for fellow cancer patients was evident in the solidarity she demonstrated during the darkest period of her life.

Rebekah was due to have six rounds of chemotherapy, but after only the third round, her fighting spirit prevailed. As she was going into her 4th round of chemo, the doctor told her the joyous news that it was due to be her last – it seemed as if her body was winning the battle against cancer!

It was confirmed a month later — the doctor told her the good news that she was in remission. She had beaten cancer!

It didn't take long before she was back on the pitch. She played again for the Bulleen Lions only 348 days after making her last appearance for Brighton and Hove Albion. While some people go a lifetime with not much achieved, in the space of a year, Stott had not only played for two professional teams but also beaten cancer and inspired millions of people with her story of grit and determination.

The crowning glory for Stott arrived in 2023 when she stepped onto the field in her homeland to represent her country at the pinnacle of any player's career: the World Cup. Although the Ferns didn't achieve the desired outcome in their home tournament, becoming the first host nation to be eliminated from the Women's World Cup at the group stage, Rebekah Stott had already attained the most significant victory among all the women participating in that event. With a smile and a consistent high spirit, she triumphed over one of the greatest adversaries on our planet — inspiring an entire generation of men and women to dream big when faced with life's scariest challenge.

Stott's dream is only getting better. At the time of writing, she has been awarded the captaincy of her football team, Melbourne City — a testament to her grit and passion. This newfound lease of life has only fuelled her determination to make an even greater impact on the millions of girls worldwide who dream of achieving success in football.

CHAPTER 30
FORMIGA — FORMIDABLE FOR AGES

How does one even *begin* telling the story of the one player who's played international football for the most time? It would only seem fitting to begin at the very start...

Miraildes Maciel Mota was born in 1978 in Salvador, Brazil, into a family of four siblings. She was the only girl, and her father died when she was eight months old.

Her mother raised the family — and by osmosis perhaps, Miraildes picked up a relentless work ethic from her that would define her career. A work ethic of such epic proportions that it would see her become one of the giants of the game — metaphorically, of course, as she only stands at 5" 4 (163cm).

Despite being born when it was *illegal* for women to play football in Brazil, Miraildes fell in love with football from an early age. She would often join her brothers whenever they played ball on the streets of Bahia. Unfortunately for her, she didn't have the same love from her brothers as many of the other football players in this book had. Her brothers often told her to "go back home to wash dishes," as they couldn't stand the thought of their sister playing football with them, let alone playing *better* than them - which she often did!

Fortunately for Miraildes (and countless generations of girls she has inspired), she never allowed herself to be deterred by her brothers' ignorant remarks. Encouraged by her mother's unwavering support, she persevered through the hurtful gender stereotyping comments hurled at her by her own family. She remained steadfast in her pursuit of her dreams.

In the streets of Salvador, Miraildes began to display the bravery that defied her young age, and that would come to characterise her career. As a little girl, she would frequently knock on her neighbours' doors, inviting other girls to join her in playing football. However, her friends' response was often hesitant and filled with apprehension. "Are you crazy?! My dad would kill me!" they would exclaim.

Despite the societal disapproval of girls playing football, Miraildes was determined not to let anything stop her from pursuing her number one passion. She refused to let the silly stereotypes dictate her dreams, knowing in her heart that they were just that: silly.

Miraildes had a progressive attitude toward life and a remarkable football brain. Even from a young age, she demonstrated an unparalleled ability to read a game of football. While her exceptional football IQ would later lead to the longest international career in football history, her relentless determination on the field earned her the nickname "Formiga," which means 'ant' in her native Portuguese. This nickname was given to her by a spectator who witnessed her play at the tender age of 13. Miraildes' tireless coverage of every blade of grass on the pitch that day was so remarkable that the spectator likened her work ethic to that of an ant. "Formiga" then stuck for life.

Formiga's career took off when she was 17 and called up for Brazil's World Cup squad of 1995. It was the beginning of a seemingly endless career. The following year, she would appear in the Atlanta 96 Olympics, the first time that women's football appeared at the Olympics. At the time of writing, there has *never* been a Women's Olympic Football competition in which Formiga has not taken part, and Atlanta 96 was over 27 years ago!

Formiga's remarkable work ethic not only earned her a nickname but also propelled her to unprecedented achievements in football. Her ability to read the game and her exceptional fitness allowed her to make history as the only player to feature in seven World Cups and seven Olympic Games. Formiga amassed an impressive 234 international caps before retiring in 2021.

Formiga epitomises the essence of football as a team game. Despite hailing from Brazil, a nation known for producing extraordinary football players, her longevity is a testament to the power of teamwork. She illustrates that the greatest football teams excel because they operate as cohesive units, greater than the sum of their individual parts — even when they include the longest-serving international player in global football!

In a country where the football federation favours the men's team over the women's team (not too dissimilar to The Reggae Girlz we spoke about in Chapter 3), Formiga has ensured her everlasting presence leaves a mark on the women's game in Brazil. Her name can be uttered in the same sentences as other Brazilian legends like Pelé, Ronaldo, and Marta.

Formiga's fearless approach to the game started as a young girl when she invited other girls in her street to play football with her. Willing to break conventions at that age, that visionary outlook continued throughout her career. It allowed her to become the most capped player in Brazilian history. Despite retiring from international football at 43, Formiga's legacy off the field is poised to have an even longer-lasting impact than her illustrious playing career.

Her story and journey serve as an inspiration not only to millions of girls worldwide but also to men, especially her own brothers. In a delightful twist of fate, witnessing Formiga's relentless drive to the pinnacle of world football has turned her brothers into her biggest fans!

CHAPTER 31
RAFAELLE SOUZA — REPRESENTING THE DREAMS OF MILLIONS

Like many Brazilian football stars, Rafaelle's journey began by kicking a ball up and down some of Brazil's poorest streets. Barefoot and hungry, her love for football made her childhood happier than what her surrounding conditions ought to have made it.

Growing up in Cipo, Bahia, Rafaelle lived and breathed football. It wasn't until she was ten that she began thinking about turning what she loved into a profession. However, her dreams were quickly extinguished when she realised there were no women who played football—after all, all the people she saw on TV playing the game were men.

She had never seen a women's game and was convinced a professional women's team didn't exist. Nevertheless, the pull and love for the game she loved was so strong that she continued playing football with other boys, undeterred by the fact that Rafaelle thought she'd never become a professional football player.

That all changed for Rafaelle on a late September morning in 2007 when she turned on her television and found herself watching Formiga (Chapter 30) on TV. The Brazilian national broadcaster was showing the Women's World Cup final on TV. Formiga and her teammates were in China battling against Germany to see who would become world champions. This proved one of the two most pivotal moments in Rafaelle's life.

Brazil would go on to lose the game, but their loss would become a small victory for thousands of girls nationwide. Girls like Rafaelle, who didn't even know women could play competitive football, let alone represent their *country* in the final of a World Cup! This was the power of representation at its very finest.

Seeing girls like her compete at the highest level propelled Rafaelle to take action. Especially after seeing Marta playing for Brazil, as she came from Alagoas, just next to Bahia, the state Rafaelle lived in.

It wasn't long before she found herself playing for Sao Francisco do Conde in Salvador before being offered a football scholarship at the University of Mississippi. Excelling in the USA, she scored 44 goals in 61 games for her university and earned a degree in Civil Engineering. Her achievements showcased her ability to succeed both on and off the field, demonstrating that whatever Rafaelle set her mind to, she would accomplish.

Due to the lack of financial support shown to the women's game, and buoyed by her academic success, Rafaelle was frighteningly close to accepting a job straight out of university.

"I was going to go into engineering because I could make more money than playing football in Brazil," Souza told the BBC.

Luckily for the women's game, and this is the second pivotal moment in Rafaelle's Life, Changchun Zhuoyue Football Club came knocking on her door with a lucrative offer to play in the Chinese Women's Super League. This fast-tracked her trajectory onto the world stage, and it wasn't long before she started playing for Arsenal FC in England, becoming the first Brazilian woman to don the Gunners' shirt.

Having seen Formiga play in the 2007 World Cup Final, Rafaelle found herself playing alongside 'The Ant' for Brazil only four years later. She made her debut for Brazil in 2011 and, together with Formiga and Marta, formed the backbone of a team that would inspire millions of girls in Brazil, the spiritual home of football.

Rafaelle won the Copa America Femenina twice and helped Arsenal win the Women's League Cup in 2023. As a no-nonsense defender, clinching the Copa America in 2022 without conceding a single goal will be one of Rafaelle's most significant accomplishments. However, her legacy will be forged by something bigger than any individual trophies.

She has ascended through the international ranks and currently captains the Brazilian football team. From a 16-year-old who didn't even know women *could* play football, she now carries the mantle of representation, inspiring young girls across her country to dream of becoming professional football stars from an early age.

With every kick of the ball and every tough tackle on the field, she demonstrates that dreams of making it professionally shouldn't be restricted to young boys in Brazil but that their female peers on the school playground can also aspire to achieve the same dreams!

Rafaelle's journey began in 2007 when she witnessed the world's best-ever player representing her country on TV. In an extraordinary turn of events, not only did she replicate those achievements, but within a few years of seeing her country's team on TV, she went on to captain a Brazil side that included the world's best-ever player. Rafaelle's unwavering drive and tenacity to pursue her dreams, along with her role as captain of a team that featured the world's greatest-ever player, undoubtedly earns her a worthy mention in this book.

But who is the greatest player ever? Well, I'm glad you asked.

CHAPTER 32
MARTA — IMMORTAL

"CRY IN THE BEGINNING SO YOU CAN SMILE IN THE END." THOSE were the impassioned words of Marta Vieira Da Silva to women across Brazil as they crashed out of the 2019 World Cup.

She was desperate for more women in her country to follow in her footsteps and revive a Brazilian team failing to attract younger girls into the squad.

Marta's story is marked by incredible hardship and a relentless battle against stereotypes and inequality. And like so many of the inspirational women in this book, her journey was shaped by the influence of her mother.

Born in 1986 and growing up in rural Brazil, Marta would wake up every morning with a tireless desire to go outside and play football. She would have this burning passion despite being different — she would be surrounded by a sea of boys whenever she played — all boys, not *one* girl.

Marta's mother often left her and her three siblings

to their own devices. As a single mum, she worked hard to support the family – she wouldn't return home until later in the evening after the sun had gone down. When she returned to her neighbourhood, she would be confronted by outraged neighbours complaining about Marta's actions during the day.

"What has she done?" was the first thing Marta's mum would ask the irate neighbours.

It turns out Marta's only misdemeanour was to play football with the boys. Nevertheless, her mother was bombarded with complaints when she got home after hours of working hard:

"Why are you letting her play a man's game?"

"What is a girl doing running around with boys?"

"What is she trying to prove?"

Luckily for Marta, her mother brushed aside all the negative talk and encouraged her daughter to pursue the sport she loved. Marta didn't mind getting called names or being picked on by bullies; she loved the sport too much. Her audacity to fight when many others would give up propelled her to become one of the greatest players on earth. While she was undoubtedly hurt by the abuse thrown her way, Marta found strength in her mother's support to continue pursuing her passion.

Inspired by her mum's relentless dedication to their family, Marta mirrored this tenacity on football pitches worldwide. If her mum could wake up at 5 a.m., work an entire shift, and return home at 8 p.m. to cook and care for the family, then nothing on the field could compare in terms of gruelling effort. This mentality made Marta thrive!

At 14 years old, Marta stopped playing barefoot on the backstreets of Alagoas when Brazilian football club Vasco da Gama gave her her first professional contract. She would impress so much that within a couple of years, she was playing for Santa Cruz in Brazil. Before she knew it, she was on a flight to Sweden to play for Umeå IK.

In Sweden, the young girl from Brazil transformed into a global phenomenon. Over four years with the club, she made 103 appearances, scoring an incredible 111 goals. That's more than a goal per game while wearing the black jersey of UIK!

The world had never seen a female football player with such an abundance of natural talent. Marta could glide past any opponent with effortless ease – her strong build defying the speed at which she easily dribbled past defenders. People inevitably compared her to her Brazilian male counterparts Ronaldinho and Rivaldo, both of whom had been Marta's idols as she grew up, particularly because Rivaldo was also left-footed like her.

There was a slight difference, however. Ronaldinho and Rivaldo each won one Ballon d'Or while Marta won SIX! Five of which were in a row! The dominance Marta had in the women's game was unparalleled. No other athlete in the sport has even come close to maintaining their status as the best for so long. Lionel Messi came close, but even the male G.O.A.T. only managed to win the Ballon d'Or award four times in a row.

Dribble after dribble and goal after goal, Marta showed the world between 2006 and 2010 that she was the undisputed heavyweight champion of world football - her pinnacle coming at the 2007 Women's World Cup, where she scored seven goals to become the Golden Boot of the tournament. Brazil defeated the U.S.A. (the favourites to win the tournament) 4-0 in the semi-final to set up a clash with Germany. Although they lost 2-0 at the showpiece event, it didn't stop Marta from being named the tournament's best player and taking the Golden Ball with her. She had become a global phenomenon at the peak of her powers!

Back home, and thanks to Marta, Brazilians were finally taking note of the women's national football team after years of neglect. Marta was suddenly being compared to Pelé, the greatest Brazilian male player ever to play the sport. Pelé himself called Marta "Pelé with a skirt," - which was not only disrespectful to a player who arguably was as good, if not better than him, but it also showed that there were more significant battles to be won in the race to rid the world of unnecessary stereotypes like those of women being portrayed in skirts.

That didn't faze Marta. Her stranglehold on the world stage started when she was only 17 years old and would last for decades. She would mesmerise millions of girls worldwide for many years to come.

In the 2019 World Cup, she scored her 17th World Cup goal, making her the all-time World Cup highest goal scorer in both men's and women's competitions, surpassing Miroslav Klose's all-time record of 16 goals in

4 tournaments. Marta had not only become the all-time World Cup goal scorer but also the first football player of any gender to score at five World Cups, a feat which, in the men's game, has only recently been matched by Cristiano Ronaldo.

Marta's flair and technical ability also impacted Olympic Football. At the 2020 Olympics, she became the first football player to score a goal in *five* consecutive Olympics, earning her country a silver medal in Athens 2004 and Beijing 2008.

The greatest on-the-field accolade that can be given to Marta is that she was named Women's Player of the Year, a record 6 times, despite never winning any major honours for her country. In a sport where most recognition is given after a major trophy victory, it speaks volumes of Marta's skill and ability.

However, the greatest tribute to Marta is acknowledging the legacy she leaves behind off the field. She is a beacon of hope for all girls striving to pursue their football passion, especially in towns and cities where girls' teams have yet to emerge. Her journey inspires countless women globally who face discrimination due to their love for The Beautiful Game. Marta's relentless drive to pursue her love for the sport is a powerful reminder that perseverance and dedication make anything possible.

A fearless leader on and off the field, Marta shed more tears in the early days of her career than most professionals ever do. Yet, those tears were not shed in vain. They were shed as a testament to her determined persistence to pave a smoother path for future generations of girls who will follow in her footsteps. Marta's tears were a sacrifice, a symbol of the struggles she endured so that others may face fewer obstacles. She cried not for herself but for the promise of brighter tomorrows for those who dare to dream. And as a role model shattering barriers, Marta showed us all that through hard work and tenacity, we can rise above our challenges and emerge victorious. In the end, her tears gave way to radiant smiles for women worldwide — the smiles of triumph, of resilience, and of hope for a better tomorrow.

AFTERWORD

As we take a moment to soak in the incredible journeys shared on these pages, it hits home just how impactful these women have been beyond the football field. And just how similar all their journeys have been. Their stories inspire change and motivate people from all walks of life to chase their dreams fearlessly and challenge the norms. They show us that barriers are there to be smashed through, stereotypes are made to be shattered, and dreams are worth chasing with all our might.

As we wrap up this adventure through the history of women's football, let's remember the valuable lessons and inspiring tales we've heard. We must keep pushing boundaries, defying expectations, and standing up for gender equality in sports. Most importantly, let's hope that the stories shared in this book light a fire in the hearts of future female football stars, referees, managers, sports commentators, or any field within football that they want to pursue, reminding them that passion, grit, and self-belief can make anything possible both on and off the pitch.

Here's to these incredible women whose stories have the power to fuel the dreams of everyone who reads them. May they inspire each and every one of us to dream big, aim high, and make our own unforgettable mark on the world of football.

ACKNOWLEDGMENTS

I want to give a special shoutout to Verity Hayhow for her amazing work on the cover design and illustrations. And a big thank you to Sophie for her incredible support – it means the world to me.

ABOUT THE AUTHOR

Michael Langdon is an accomplished writer and a seasoned attendee of five World Cups, showcasing his deep-rooted passion for football. He embarked on his football journey by coaching youth football in the United States, laying the foundation for his future endeavours.

After attaining best-selling status with his book "Welcome to the Age of Emotion," Michael's focus shifted to his greatest passion: football. This marked the inception of his groundbreaking work, "The Most Amazing Football Stories of All Time," a testament to his dedication and love for the sport.

Michael has achieved remarkable success as a multi-award-winning video producer and best-selling author. He has faithfully followed his beloved England team at the past five World Cups and regularly indulges in Saturday afternoons at The Amex stadium in Sussex, watching Brighton & Hove Albion exceed expectations.

In addition to his writing prowess, Michael is an experienced media commentator renowned for his insightful videos that have generated millions of dollars for e-commerce sites. His expertise has earned him recognition in esteemed publications like The Huffington Post and Mashable. As the founder and Managing

Director of Levity, Michael's client roster boasts top-tier e-commerce companies and global giants such as TikTok, Facebook, and Speedo.

Michael dedicates most of his time to his football publishing career, nurturing his passion for the sport and sharing captivating stories with his readers.

Connect with the author:

Instagram: @Itsmikelangdon

TikTok: @Itsmikelangdon

Facebook: @Iammlangdon

Printed in Great Britain
by Amazon